Herman Melville

Titles in the series Critical Lives present the work of leading cultural figures of the modern period. Each book explores the life of the artist, writer, philosopher or architect in question and relates it to their major works.

In the same series

Herman Melville

Kevin J. Hayes

REAKTION BOOKS

In honour of Jay Leyda

Published by Reaktion Books Ltd
Unit 32, Waterside
44–48 Wharf Road
London N1 7UX, UK

www.reaktionbooks.co.uk

First published 2017
Copyright © Kevin J. Hayes 2017

Printed and bound in Great Britain by Bell & Bain, Glasgow

A catalogue record for this book is available from the British Library

ISBN 978 1 78023 807 4

Contents

Herman Melville, photographic print, *c.* 1860.

Introduction

The London socialite Winifride Wrench once attended a luncheon where she met a man who told her about Herman Melville and *Moby-Dick*. Never before had she heard the author's name or the book's title, but the man's enthusiasm was infectious. Reading *Moby-Dick*, he claimed, could change a person forever. She soon bought a copy for herself. Recalling the moment, Wrench did not say precisely when the luncheon occurred, but she dated it to early 1921. The date makes sense. At the time W. K. Kelsey, an American journalist, called *Moby-Dick* 'the greatest sensation of the winter in London'.[1]

In coffeehouses and club rooms and pubs and drawing rooms, *Moby-Dick* was the talk of the town. Wherever literary people gathered, according to Kelsey, one could overhear their conversation: 'Have you read *Moby-Dick*? I say, old man, ginger up a bit and read it.' The British journalist H. M. Tomlinson joined a group of London businessmen at a suburban home one cold winter night to discuss *Moby-Dick*, which, to his surprise and delight, they did with animation and wonder. A banker compared Melville's prose to Shakespearean tragedy: *Moby-Dick* made him think of *Macbeth*.[2]

British readers were talking about Melville partly because Oxford University Press republished *Moby-Dick* in late 1920 as part of its Oxford World's Classics series. This 'small green closely printed volume', as Wrench described her new copy of the Oxford *Moby-Dick*, generated more interest than any other title previously published in the series. In his regular column for *New Age* in the last week of September 1921, Herbert Read called Oxford's publication of *Moby-Dick* 'an event to be annalled'. Two months later the English editor Lewis Hind admitted, 'It is this World's Classics edition that we have all been reading.'[3] The attention the Oxford *Moby-Dick* received cannot be attributed solely to the publisher's marketing. Historical and cultural factors created the conditions necessary for the Melville revival.

The changes the world had undergone since the mid-nineteenth century made people amenable to Melville's writings. For those living in 1851, the year he first published *Moby-Dick*, the world seemed more and more legible. Physiognomy, phrenology, graphology: all these supposed sciences scrutinized people's external aspects – facial features, cranial contours, chirographic curlicues – as signs revealing the inner self. Legibility provided comfort, letting people see the world for what it was. Potential threats – murder, evil, madness – telegraphed warning signs. A belief in progress and human perfectibility ruled. People genuinely thought the world was getting better.

Melville did not share the prevailing optimism. He knew that the world is not as legible as it seems, that the advance of civilization does not necessarily mean progress, that evil is part of nature. Contemporary readers had difficulty appreciating Melville's work partly because they had difficulty understanding his worldview. The way people viewed the world after the Great War more closely coincided with Melville's perspective. Suddenly the planet was a much scarier place. All those external features were not signs of the inner self but masks misleading anyone who tried to penetrate them. Pessimism replaced optimism. After the war the concept of all-pervasive evil no longer appeared far-fetched.

Literary history follows a similar narrative arc. Content in their beliefs, mid-nineteenth-century readers disliked literature with an unrecognizable form. They didn't want surprises. They wanted to know what they would be reading before they read it. Melville's daring stylistic innovations were difficult for his contemporaries to take. Michael Sadleir included a Melville section in *Excursions in Victorian Bibliography* (1922) – another sign of the revival – but admitted that he hardly seemed Victorian: 'If he belongs to any period or to any genealogy, [Melville] is of the ageless, raceless family of the lonely giants.'[4]

Not until the modernist era would the experimental quality of Melville's writing find a truly appreciative audience. Oxford republished *Moby-Dick* the same time D. H. Lawrence published *Women in Love*, two years before T. S. Eliot issued *The Waste Land* and James Joyce released *Ulysses*. *Moby-Dick* suited modernism remarkably well. Soon after Joyce's masterpiece appeared, Leonard Woolf compared it with Melville's: '*Ulysses* . . . both in style and conception continually recalls *Moby-Dick*.'[5]

Tomlinson, who first learned about *Moby-Dick* from a friend who had gone insane during the Somme, was unsure how to interpret what his friend told him about the book: his extravagant praise seemed like another manifestation of mental illness. Having served as a war correspondent at the Somme, Tomlinson himself returned from that sad and bloody battlefield plagued with never-ending nightmares of its horror. He doubted whether *Moby-Dick* could do anything to lift his spirits or mend his soul, to take the edge off razor-sharp memories of death and disfigurement. He was wrong, as he discovered for himself:

> I set out, with small hope, with Ahab after Moby Dick. I was at once caught in an awful adventure in which men, ships, seas, harpoons, and Leviathan are but dread symbols, and in a sense I have never returned from that trip. I became missing as soon as the *Pequod* was out of sight of Nantucket. While the book was unfinished there was no home, there were no duties, and time and space were figments. It was an immense experience.[6]

Melville's masterpiece opened a new vista for Tomlinson. It showed him that the world, no matter how dark and violent, could still lend itself to art.

Moby-Dick astonished many other readers in post-war London. In a period of a single week Tomlinson spoke with several of the city's leading writers and editors – Arnold Bennett, H. W. Massingham, John Middleton Murry, Frank Swinnerton – all of whom proclaimed *Moby-Dick* 'to be the – well to be IT. There ain't nothing like it. There never will be again.'[7] Tomlinson's friends did more than talk about *Moby-Dick*, they also wrote about it. Bennett and Swinnerton, who often lunched together at the Reform Club, happened to discuss *Moby-Dick* at the club one day shortly after the Oxford edition appeared. Together they decided to 'convince the world that *Moby-Dick* was the greatest of all sea-novels'.[8]

Interest in Melville crossed political boundaries. Massingham, editor of the radical *Nation*, grouped the author of *Moby-Dick* with Rabelais, Swift and Shakespeare, advising 'any adventurer of the soul to go at once into the morose and prolonged retreat necessary for its deglutition'. J. C. Squire, editor of the conservative *London Mercury*, commented, 'I do not believe that there exists a greater work of prose fiction in English than *Moby-Dick*.'[9]

With the critical and commercial success of the Oxford *Moby-Dick*, Sadleir prepared an edition of Melville's collected works, which Constable issued in a finely printed and beautifully bound sixteen-volume edition over the next three years. The Constable edition brought other works to the attention of English readers. Speaking about Melville's fourth book, based on his youthful voyage to Liverpool aboard a merchant ship, John St Loe Strachey said, 'How well worth reading is *Redburn*.' Surprised and charmed by *Israel Potter* – Melville's foray into historical romance – Arthur Wallace especially enjoyed the scene in Paris where Benjamin Franklin introduces the book's eponymous hero to John Paul Jones: 'As an exercise in whimsical character study in a historic setting the conversation of this ill-assorted trio has not been bettered.' John Middleton Murry enjoyed *Billy Budd*, which he called 'the last will and spiritual testament of a man of genius'.[10]

The list goes on. Leonard Woolf grouped *Mardi* with *Moby-Dick*, arguing that Melville's reputation must stand or fall on the basis of these, his two most ambitious books. Each achieves 'a higher plane of fantastic grandeur and poetry where even the intolerable rantings and ravings find a proper place'. Bennett also recognized Melville's modernity, observing that the author of *Pierre* attempts what 'the most advanced novelists of today imagine to be quite new'. Bennett admitted *Pierre* was not for everyone: 'I recommend it exclusively to the adventurous and the fearless. These, if the book does not defeat them, will rise up, after recovering from their exhaustion, and thank me.'[11]

Reviewing the Constable edition, Strachey supplied his own recommendation: 'No library, public or private, that professes to represent English literature can possibly be without it.'[12] Strachey's classification of Melville's work as English literature may seem odd, but he chose his words carefully. As editor of *The Spectator*, Strachey had often stressed the political and cultural ties between the United States and Great Britain. Melville's writings were English literature because they were written in the language the two nations shared.

Strachey was not the only one to hold this view. Squire, as general editor of Macmillan's English Men of Letters, chose Melville as the subject and John Freeman as the author of the initial volume for a new set of titles in the series. Released in 1926, Freeman's *Herman Melville* was the first book about Melville published in England. Macmillan also issued Freeman's book in New York, though his preface appears with an extra sentence not present in the London edition: 'I hope America will pardon the inclusion of an American writer among English Men of Letters.'[13]

Winifride Wrench joined all the editors, journalists and novelists writing critical appreciations of *Moby-Dick* during the early 1920s. Her essay shows that not only did she start reading Melville's works, but she read Melville criticism. She quotes 'The Whiteness of the Whale', arguably the finest chapter in the book, and cites Squire's comment about *Moby-Dick* being the greatest work of prose fiction in the English language. Her essay appeared in *Landmark*, the journal her brother, Sir Evelyn Wrench, edited. *Landmark* was the official organ of the English-Speaking Union, which Sir Evelyn had founded to promote friendship and cooperation between the British Empire and the United States. His sister's essay advances the organization's goals. Concluding her discussion, Winifride Wrench observed, 'He has come into his own at last; wherever the English language is read, there will the discerning reader worship at Melville's shrine.'[14]

Melville's impact soon stretched beyond the English-speaking world. Though his first two books, *Typee* and *Omoo*, had been translated into German shortly after their original release, *Moby-Dick*, beyond a few excerpts in French, had not been translated. Once British readers revived interest in Melville, people from other nations became interested. In 1927 *Moby-Dick* appeared in an abridged German translation. Finnish and French translations followed the next year, with Dutch, Hungarian and Polish versions by the end of the decade.[15] Translations into several other languages would appear before the Second World War, and essayists across Europe began publishing critical appreciations of *Moby-Dick* and other Melville works.

France provides a good illustration of how the word spread. Some of the leading French critics of Melville's day – Philarète Chasles, E.-D. Forgues, Joseph Milsand – greeted his work enthusiastically.[16] Forgues, who initiated the French appreciation of Edgar Allan Poe in the 1840s, took it upon himself to translate some excerpts of *Moby-Dick* for *Revue des deux mondes*. French readers did not cotton to Melville as they had to Poe. Not until 1926 was *Typee* published in French, with a *Moby-Dick* translation two years later.

Neither had much impact. Issued as *Le Cachalot blanc*, the 1928 French translation of *Moby-Dick* was designed for young readers. An illustrated quarto edition appeared the following year, but otherwise the French expressed little interest in Melville before the mid-1930s, when Pierre Leyris, an ambitious young translator who would take it upon himself to render many great books into French, turned his attention to Melville, issuing translations of *Billy Budd* (1935), *Benito Cereno* (1937) and *Pierre* (1939).

Not until Gallimard published *Moby-Dick* in 1941 in a translation by Lucien Jacques, Joan Smith and Jean Giono did French enthusiasm for Melville truly erupt. As both a heartfelt homage and a clever marketing device Giono published *Pour saluer Melville*, a novel paying tribute to Melville's life and writings. Reprinted dozens of times, the Gallimard *Moby-Dick* elicited critical appreciations from some of France's finest thinkers.

Reviewing the Gallimard translation, Maurice Blanchot found *Moby-Dick* a great work of universal literature, a 'total book' that 'not only expressed a complete human experience, but also presented itself as the written equivalent of the universe'.[17] Jean-Paul Sartre also reviewed the Gallimard *Moby-Dick*. He argued that 'The Whiteness of the Whale' anticipated the latest literary trends:

> No one except Melville has attempted this extraor-
> dinary undertaking: to retain the indefinable taste of a
> pure quality – the purest quality, whiteness – and seek
> in that taste itself the absolute which goes beyond it.
> If this is a direction contemporary literature is groping
> toward, then Melville is the most 'modern' writer.[18]

The Gallimard edition appeared when Albert Camus was sketching out ideas for his next novel, *The Plague*. One chapter, 'The Jeroboam's Story', was a seedbed for Camus, telling the story of a whaleship struck by a malignant epidemic, and a delusional crew member named Gabriel who exploits the pestilence to gain power over the superstitious foremastmen.[19] Jean-Pierre Grumbach, to cite one further example, was a member of the French Resistance. Inspired by *Moby-Dick*, he used 'Jean-Pierre Melville' as his *nom de guerre*. In other words the man who created Captain Ahab lent his name to a man who combatted tyranny. The Frenchman liked his *nom de guerre* so well he kept it *après la guerre*, when Jean-Pierre Melville emerged as a leading film-maker. Henceforth the author of *The Confidence-Man* and the director of *Bob le flambeur* would share the same last name.

From country to country and language to language, *Moby-Dick* captured the attention of readers around the globe. Whereas Herman Melville had slipped into obscurity by the start of the twentieth century, by its end he had achieved recognition as a leader of world literature. Though his story has been told many times before, it deserves to be retold. The ongoing conversion of print material into digital form has created almost limitless possibilities for exploration. Despite its brevity, the present work incorporates a wealth of new information to retell the story of the man whom many consider the finest author his nation has produced.

1

Schools and Schoolmasters

The *Adonis* reached New York on 31 August 1818, having left Le Havre less than four weeks earlier. The passengers included Allan Melvill, as the family then spelled its name. The cargo included fancy French goods he had acquired in Paris: kid gloves, silk stockings, cambric handkerchiefs, tortoiseshell combs and more. Planning to establish a new wholesale importing business in Manhattan, he could not fit everything on the *Adonis* and arranged for a later ship, the *Marcus*, to carry the rest. Less than three weeks after the *Adonis* arrived, Allan Melvill opened a French goods store at 123 Pearl Street.[1]

Newspaper advertisements indicate the store opened in mid-September, not November, as previous biographies contend.[2] This new information shows Melvill had different priorities from those formerly assumed. Entering the mercantile business in Boston sixteen years earlier, he had undervalued a shipment he sold to a wily entrepreneur named Sampson Wilder.[3] Melvill now moved more quickly to get his goods on the market. When he returned from France this time, his store was his top priority. His son Herman was conceived around 1 November 1818. In other words Melvill opened his store before he conceived his son.

Since boyhood Allan Melvill had tried hard to live up to his lineage. Though he could trace his roots to Scottish lairds, he did not need to go any further on the family tree than his father to find a distinguished ancestor. Major Thomas Melvill was a rebel who had participated in the Boston Tea Party and who preserved some tea leaves from the event in a small green-glass vial, which the family cared for 'with as much holy reverence as the miraculous robes of St Bridget by the superstitious believer of the anti-Protestant faith'.[4] Allan wished to succeed in business, not necessarily for the wealth it promised but for the accompanying social prestige. His reading reflects his quest for social standing: Lord Chesterfield's *Principles of Politeness*, for example taught him how to be a gentleman.[5] Allan Melvill's ongoing fascination with conduct literature reflects his obsession with what others thought about him.

Unable to purchase all the books he wished to read, Allan Melvill patronized the circulating library at the Boston Book Store. Though its proprietors advertised that the collection contained a variety of useful books, it differed little from other circulating libraries: novels and romances predominated.[6] Serious readers looked down their noses at the novel. The bias against fiction would persist for decades, a stumbling block for Allan's son Herman.

The plan to establish a new library in Boston, one catering to a more exclusive clientele than the circulating libraries, appealed to Allan Melvill. The Boston Athenaeum sought to assemble a collection of great works of learning and science. In 1807 he became one of its original subscribers.[7] As a member he could satisfy his personal goals of self-improvement and social prestige. The Boston Athenaeum provided access to books, and people, of quality.

His search for new business opportunities took Allan to Albany, where, in 1813, he met Maria Gansevoort, whose family was possibly the city's wealthiest. Did Allan Melvill court the Gansevoort daughter to get the Gansevoort dollars? Perhaps – but Maria had something else many wealthy young women did not: a father who was a Revolutionary war hero. General Peter Gansevoort, who had passed away the previous year, was best known for defeating the British forces at Fort Stanwix, which turned the tide of the war in upstate New York. By connecting himself with the Gansevoorts,

Thomas Melvill, 19th-century engraving.

Allan Melvill could enhance his social standing and give his
children another heroic grandfather to admire.

After their wedding on 4 October 1814, Allan and Maria
Melvill moved into the Gansevoort home on Market Street with
General Gansevoort's widow Catherine and her youngest son, Peter
Gansevoort Jr. Allan found a position with a wholesale dry goods
business in Albany. Their first child, a boy, was born on

John Francis Eugene Prudhomme, *Peter Gansevoort*, steel engraving, modelled on the portrait of Herman Melville's grandfather by Gilbert Stuart that hung in the Gansevoorts' Albany home during Herman's youth.

7 December 1815. They named him Gansevoort. Helen Maria, their second child, was born on 4 August 1817. Six more children would follow at roughly two-year intervals.

Reading to improve himself, Allan acquired *Melancholy: As It Proceeds from the Disposition and Habit, the Passion of Love, and the Influence of Religion*.[8] The book stemmed from Robert Burton's *Anatomy of Melancholy*, which would profoundly influence Herman's writing. The acquisition might seem intellectually ambitious, but the edition is a nineteenth-century redaction that turned Burton's text into a conduct book. The original was too difficult, the editor says. Its bold metaphors, humorous observations, ingenious digressions, scattershot erudition and superabundant matter – aspects Herman would love – made it impossible to read. The editor chose snippets of Burton's text to suit his didactic purpose: to avoid melancholy through temperance, chastity and piety.

Allan tired of working for someone else and living with his controlling brother-in-law in Albany. New York, he knew, would be the nation's commercial capital. Allan loved his wife and children and hated spending time away from them, but he longed to revisit France to obtain sufficient merchandise to re-establish his business. Major Melvill, having supported his son's prior ventures, loaned him sufficient funds for this new scheme. His father's money bought the goods that filled the *Marcus* and *Adonis*.

Once he established his Manhattan business, Allan sought a home for his family. On 12 May 1819, they moved to 6 Pearl Street. Located two doors from where Pearl meets the Battery, the elegant home, which Allan could ill afford, suited the lavish lifestyle he imagined for his young family. A ten-room house with elegant marble mantelpieces, it was 'finished in the best manner and most fashionable style'.[9] Here their third child would be born. On Sunday, 1 August 1819, Maria Melvill gave birth to a healthy baby with sparkling blue eyes whom they named after his uncle, Herman Gansevoort.

To escape the threat of cholera Maria took Gansevoort, Helen and Herman to Albany the following summer. When they returned to New York in September, Allan had a surprise: a new home at 55 Courtlandt Street. A hitherto unrecorded real estate advertisement shows it was even more luxurious than the home on Pearl Street. A three-storey brick house, it had marble mantelpieces, folding doors, a brick cistern for collecting rainwater and large vaults for storage. The advertisement explains: 'This is a very convenient dwelling for a genteel family, and a desirable, pleasant and healthy situation.'[10] They would continue to move to larger and nicer homes during their time in New York, none of which Allan Melvill could afford.

Beyond an ominous joke Helen made about their father always having a hickory switch in his hand, the record is silent when it comes to documenting how he treated his children. A letter to his adolescent nephew Guert Gansevoort indicates the kind of advice Allan Melvill gave youngsters. When Guert first sailed as a midshipman in 1823, Uncle Allan wrote him a clever letter of advice:

> You are now fairly launched at an early age upon the great Ocean of life . . . with Honour for a compass, and Glory for a watch word, you may in peace or war, become a brave and accomplished naval Officer . . . inculcate obedience, patriotism, fortitude and temperance.[11]

Allan's letter echoes his conduct manuals. He gave Guert one to take aboard: *A Guide to Men and Manners*, a compendium of advice from such works as Chesterfield's *Letters to His Son* and Benjamin Franklin's *Way to Wealth*. Herman came to know the conduct literature well enough to parody it. He would spoof Chesterfield on several occasions. In *Israel Potter*, for example, he observes that

> where modest gentlemanhood is all on one side, it is a losing affair; as if my Lord Chesterfield should take off his hat, and smile, and bow, to a mad bull, in hopes of a reciprocation of politeness.[12]

Elsewhere in *Israel Potter* he satirizes the idea of a sailor taking Franklin's *Way to Wealth* to sea, having John Paul Jones say, 'I must get me a copy of this, and wear it around my neck for a charm.'[13]

Herman started school when he was five. The first school he attended is unknown. It did not tax his energies, which he channelled into pestering his big brother. Gansevoort complained to their mother, saying he could not stand to be 'plagued by such a little Fellow'.[14] Once Herman developed a fondness for books, he had more material with which to tease his siblings. Helen remembered that the witches' words from *Macbeth* formed one of his favourite boyhood quotations. He would annoy his sisters with the gross lines listing what the witches placed in their boiling cauldron: 'Eye of newt, and toe of frog, / Wool of bat, and tongue of dog'.[15] While committing favourite lines to memory, Herman did not read Shakespeare thoroughly in his youth. He always had delicate eyes, and most editions of Shakespeare had tiny print.

In September 1825 the Melvills enrolled Gansevoort and Herman in New York High School. Located on Crosby Street between Grande and Broome, it was a large, three-storey brick building designed for the education of gentlemen's sons. The term 'high school' meant any school providing advanced education for older children regardless of whether it also provided elementary education. New York High School had three departments: introductory, junior and senior. In the introductory division, elementary students learned spelling, reading, writing, geography, natural history and arithmetic. To these standard subjects headmaster John Griscom added drawing lessons and taught students to appreciate art. Herman would retain a passion for art all his life.[16]

Griscom, a great believer in physical education, had gymnastic apparatus installed in the schoolyard: 'exercising bars, a climbing ladder, and in a special ground by itself and facing Broadway a flying trapeze for the use of the boys'.[17] As an adult, Herman would amaze friends with his gymnastic ability. A ship's rigging was not his first exposure to climbing apparatus. The playground of New York High School initially let him test his gymnastic skill.

Enrolment for all grades totalled around six hundred students, some of whom remained friends with Herman into adulthood, including Cornelius Mathews and Jedediah B. Auld.[18] One visitor saw four hundred students in the introductory class, all in a huge room: 'the handsomest children, as to beauty and stature, I ever beheld'.[19] Though this description is heartwarming, it begs the question: how did teachers control, let alone teach, a classroom of four hundred students? Griscom organized the school according to the monitorial system. Teachers would choose the best students as monitors, each overseeing a small group of, say, eight students. Herman achieved sufficient academic success to be chosen as a monitor in his second year.

Austin Baldwin, who superintended the introductory department, published an arithmetic textbook while Herman was his student. The textbook indicates what Herman learned as a student and what he could have taught his peers as a monitor. Baldwin understood the importance of asking questions after each lesson. He built the monitorial system into his questions. The first lesson asks, 'If you receive 10 tickets for good lessons, and 1 for being monitor, how many will you have?'[20]

Tickets constituted the school's currency. Students earned them for good performances, lost them as penalties: 'If one boy is fined 5 tickets, and another 6, how many will they both have to pay?' One question in the long-division section suits the Melvills: 'If I owe a debt of 132 dollars, and pay 12 dollars a month, how many months will it take me to pay the whole?'[21] Eleven, the correct answer, does not factor interest into the equation, but then again, the Melvills often ignored the interest on their debts.

Baldwin taught students one lesson about weights, measures and currency and another about paper, parchment and books. He taught them the different formats – folio, quarto, octavo, duodecimo – which Melville would play with in the 'Cetology' chapter of *Moby-Dick*. Baldwin also included a lesson about foreign coins that passed as current in the United States, complete with supplemental questions. Imagine Herman serving as a monitor and asking his fellow students: 'How much is a Doubloon?'[22]

After New York High School opened its doors, a similar girls'
school was erected on Crosby Street just down the block from
the boys'. The Melvills decided against sending their daughters
there, despite the fact that their father sat on the Board of Trustees
overseeing both schools.[23] What was good for the Melvill boys
was not necessarily good for the Melvill girls. Helen entered
Mrs and Miss Whieldon's French and English School, which
they operated out of Mr Whieldon's wholesale warehouse at 440
Broome Street. Mrs Whieldon and her daughter taught a variety of
subjects useful for young ladies. Mrs Whieldon taught the literary
branches of education; Miss Whieldon taught the non-literary
subjects: drawing, music, painting (on wood and velvet) and fancy
needlework.[24]

Miss Whieldon conducted a dancing academy at their Broome
Street school. She boasted about regularly receiving the latest dance
steps from England, France and Spain. Helen, who had a congenital
defect that left one leg shorter than the other, did not dance, but
Gansevoort, Herman and their sister Augusta (born two years after
Herman) attended Miss Whieldon's dancing academy. The skills
Herman developed would serve him well. He learned to dance and
to appreciate dance as an art form. In *Redburn* a shipmate expresses
anxiety about Wellingborough Redburn's dancing skills, afraid
he will disgrace them in Liverpool's dockside saloons. For sailors,
dance was a kind of language, a way to express themselves aboard
and abroad. Redburn, whose upbringing parallels his creator's,
reassures the shipmate he knows very well how to dance.[25]

Redburn also reflects its author's education. To relieve the tedium
at sea, Wellingborough Redburn repeats 'Lord Byron's Address to
the Ocean, which I had often spouted on stage at the High School at
home'. The title indicates Herman's source. He encountered Byron's
text in *The American First Class Book*, which extracts the closing
cantos from *Childe Harold's Pilgrimage* as 'Apostrophe to the Ocean'.
This anthology was designed for the highest class in school. As

an elementary student Herman was already reading at the senior high-school level.[26]

Herman read Levi W. Leonard's *Literary and Scientific Class Book* when he was nine. The *Scientific Class Book*, as students called it, covered subjects from astronomy to zoology, closing with bonus lessons about learning in general. 'The Influence of an Early Taste for Reading', a lesson presenting excerpts from the English philosopher and novelist William Godwin, celebrates the power of reading: 'He that loves reading has every thing within his reach.' Learning to read well enabled the student to read the world: 'Every object is capable of suggesting to him a volume of reflections.'[27] Godwin's words anticipate Ishmael's approach in *Moby-Dick*. Everything Ishmael encounters seems full of meaning and encourages personal reflection.

The Boatswain's Mate, another book Redburn mentions, reflects the religious literature Herman encountered in his boyhood. Despite chronic money troubles, Allan Melvill remained active in community affairs, joining the American Tract Society, which published evangelical Christian literature. *Little Henry and His Bearer*, a cloying storybook Herman would mention in the first draft of *Typee*, was one work the Society published. *The Boatswain's Mate* was another. It presents religious dialogues written in the argot of barely literate sailors. Herman questioned its value: Redburn's reference to the '*Boatswain's Mate* and other clever religious tracts in the nautical dialect' sounds decidedly facetious.[28]

Donating ten dollars towards the maintenance of the American Tract Society's New York office, Allan Melvill seems less interested in saving souls than enhancing his status. The president of the organization was Samson Wilder, the businessman who had bested him years earlier. Still trying to keep up with Wilder, Allan Melvill subsequently donated twenty dollars (equivalent to nearly seven years' tuition at New York High School) to the Tract Society, thus securing a life membership for himself.[29]

Besides continuing his studies at school, Herman, though only nine, also looked beyond the classroom walls. One Saturday in late May 1829 he left home in high spirits to ferry across the Hudson to Hoboken. The crossing only took fifteen minutes, leaving Herman nearly the whole day to explore New Jersey.[30]

A promenade led towards Elysian Fields, about a mile (1.6 km) from the ferry landing. Tall oak trees shading the promenade sometimes blocked the view, but occasional openings provided magnificent glimpses of Manhattan. Nearing Elysian Fields, the pathway gradually broadened into a meadow covered with an undulating green lawn, which provided a panoramic view of the city across the river. North from Elysian Fields, Weehawken Point juts into the river, and a brief yet steep climb leads to the top of Weehawk Hill, which offers a view of the purple Palisades, picturesque cliffs extending for several miles north along the Hudson. That Saturday Herman had time to explore everything from Hoboken to Weehawken. He did not return home until four o'clock.

While Herman was in New Jersey, his brother Gansevoort stayed home reading John Franklin's *Narrative of a Second Expedition to the Shores of the Polar Sea*. Their contrasting experiences reflect their differing personalities. Whereas Herman went exploring, Gansevoort stayed home reading a book about exploration. Herman was not necessarily against reading on Saturday: Redburn mentions 'a foggy Saturday, when schoolboys stay at home reading *Robinson Crusoe*'. But sunny Saturdays beckoned Herman outdoors. Redburn tells readers to quit their books:

If you want to learn romance, or gain an insight into things quaint, curious, and marvellous, drop your books of travel, and take a stroll along the docks of a great commercial port. Ten to one, you will encounter Crusoe himself among the crowds of mariners from all parts of the globe.[31]

That May Allan Melvill enrolled Gansevoort at the grammar school of Columbia College. The newly established school prepared some students for college and others for the mercantile trade. College-bound students took the classical course: Latin, Greek, English, mathematics and geography. Others took the English course, which omitted ancient languages but included mathematics and geography. New York High School's monitorial system poorly suited advanced subjects. Gansevoort needed more training in ancient tongues to prepare for college. Students who successfully completed the classical course at the grammar school were guaranteed admission to Columbia College. Cornelius Mathews, having transferred to the school earlier that year, would go on to Columbia. Transferring his oldest son, Allan Melvill indicated his plan to send Gansevoort to college, though he was thinking Harvard, not Columbia.[32]

Herman also wished to change schools. Allan Melvill enrolled him in the English course at Columbia Grammar School that autumn. Since Herman was three years younger than Gansevoort, his age may explain the choice. Younger boys generally took the English course. Richard Grant White, who also entered the school that autumn, took the English course. But White was only eight. Once they turned ten, many boys took the classical course. The official register of pupils enrolled at the school from mid-1828 to early 1830 shows that 23 boys entered when they were ten years old. Fourteen of them took the classical course, nine the English course.[33] Allan Melvill enrolled Herman in the English course because he planned a mercantile career for him.

When Herman started his second term at Columbia Grammar School in January 1830, a new student enrolled in the classical course. Robert Tomes was two years older than Herman, but the boys became friends. Though they were in different programmes, both took mathematics. An eager, ambitious student, Tomes would subsequently earn his MD, but literature was his passion. *My College*

John Hill, *Palisades*, 1828, aquatint based on a painting by William Guy Wall.

Days, Tomes's little-known reminiscence of his early life, provides the single fullest account of Columbia Grammar School during Herman's time there.

Mr McGorman was their mathematics teacher when Herman enrolled. 'A pompous, assuming young Irishman', McGorman, in Tomes's view, 'was, or ought to have been our teacher of arithmetic; but anything so elementary was quite too lowly for his lofty self-appreciation'. McGorman lectured 'upon the higher mathematics to a set of boys who hardly knew the multiplication table, and did not understand a word of his abstruse cogitations'.[34]

McGorman did not last at Columbia much longer. The name of his replacement has escaped history, but Tomes caricatured his physical appearance and classroom manner. He was 'tall, gaunt, and strong, with an arm as long as that of a gorilla – an animal he not only resembled in appearance but ferocity'. Gorilla Arms, Tomes explained,

wielded a cane of his own length, and slashed with it right
and left all along the benches where we poor lads sat
cowering over our slates, striking indiscriminately, regardless whom it might hit, if offender or not, like a drunken
Irishman dealing his miscellaneous blows in a row.[35]

The classroom behaviour of Gorilla Arms looks forward to the
wasp-waisted British officer in *Israel Potter*, who approaches Ethan
Allen 'flourishing his sword like a schoolmaster's ferule'.[36]

Tomes's playground memories were much happier than his
memories of mathematics. The summer before Herman enrolled,
a new building for the grammar school was erected on Murray
Street adjacent to Columbia College, but there was no access
from the grammar school. The college administrators feared
the 'boys might trample down its greensward, and commit
havoc in its smooth paths and trim shrubbery'. At recess they
played on the grammar school grounds but overflowed into
neighbouring streets during rough-and-tumble games like tag
and prisoners' base.[37]

A forerunner to baseball, prisoners' base went back to
Shakespeare's time. Richard Grant White remembered the
game when he annotated an edition of Shakespeare. Glossing an
infinitive phrase from *Venus and Adonis*, 'to bid the wind a base',
White noted that Shakespeare's diction came from prisoners' base.
To bid the wind a base meant to challenge the wind as schoolboys
challenged their opponents.[38] Prisoners' base pitted two teams
against each other. The leaders would choose sides, selecting the
fastest and most agile boys first and leaving the slow, the fat and
the gangly until last. Nine players per side was ideal. Forming a
large rectangle, the boys would mark out two bases in either corner
and two prisons opposite the bases 20 yards (18 m) distant, the
prisons of each team being catty-corner to their bases. After the
players situated themselves at their respective bases, a player from

first base would run into the centre of the rectangle to challenge the other team to a chase.

A single chase could range far and wide. The challenger simply had to return to base without being tagged. If tagged, the challenger went to prison, remaining there until a team member rescued him. The rescuer, of course, put himself in danger of being tagged and sent to prison. If the challenger returned to his base untouched, then his team would dispatch another boy to chase the chaser. Play continued until one team had sent all its adversaries to prison so that none remained to rescue them. The excitement and tension escalated as the game continued. In a vague and inchoate way prisoners' base gave Herman an inkling of the narrative possibilities of a chase.

Though the instruction at Columbia Grammar School was uneven, the student body made the time Herman and Gansevoort spent there productive and pleasurable. As a new term approached in 1830, both boys could tell they would not be going back to Columbia. More and more desperate for money, their father unloaded some prized possessions: he sold his books to feed his family.[39]

In August Allan Melvill closed his store, conducting a little remaining business from their home. No longer could he mask his failure from the older children.[40] His sons' playground game had its real-life equivalent as creditors attempted to prosecute him for non-payment. He made plans to escape them by fleeing to Albany. He sent Maria there with Helen and the younger children.[41] Three months past due on rent payments, Allan Melvill boarded the boat to Albany with Herman on 9 October 1830. A black storm delayed their departure until daybreak. The fierce weather worried Allan Melvill less than the delay. Risking arrest at any moment, he had hoped the night would cloak their escape.

Allan Melvill had sought to live the life of a gentleman. His beloved conduct manuals had told him what to do and how to act.

While facing massive debt, he had maintained a facade of gentility. All that was gone now. Though only eleven, Herman glimpsed the broken man behind the mask, a man whose profound need to maintain an aura of wealth had caused him to risk his family's welfare in the process.

Whenever the Melvills had visited Albany to see Grandmamma Gansevoort and Uncle Peter, they had stayed at the Gansevoort family home. When they moved there, Peter thought they should live separately. With the births of Frances and Thomas, their two youngest, the Melvills now had eight children. Since Catherine Gansevoort's health was declining, Peter avoided filling their home with eight little Melvills. He arranged for his sister and her family to rent a house nearby.[42] Catherine Gansevoort would succumb to illness before the year's end.

Once the family arrived in Albany and settled into their new home, Allan Melvill looked for work. Presumably aware that no salaried position would help pay his debts or support the lifestyle to which he was accustomed, he still wanted to do something. He took a job in a cap and fur store. Outside the store he pretended to be a manager, but within its walls there was no mistaking his position: a lowly clerk.[43]

Gansevoort and Herman entered Albany Academy, an imposing edifice that could either intimidate or inspire. Allan Melvill put Gansevoort in the classical course, Herman in the English course, reinforcing Herman's feelings of inferiority.[44] Allan still hoped to send Gansevoort to Harvard, without knowing how he would pay its tuition. Albany Academy placed students into different departments according to age and ability, the first being the highest. Herman started in the fourth department.

The curriculum shared similarities with Columbia Grammar School, but the teachers made all the difference. Joseph Henry, the most notable name on the faculty, would later become the driving force behind the Smithsonian Institution. At Albany

Boy's Academy, Albany, New York.

Academy Henry experimented with electromagnetic phenomena, showing students how magnets could be activated electrically over distance. A mile-long coil of wire ran round and round an upstairs classroom. The magnet at the wire's end activated a steel bar, which would strike a bell to signal the experiment's success. Though Henry discovered the scientific principle underlying the telegraph, he let Samuel Morse put the discovery to practical use.

Herman had the opportunity to witness Henry's experiments, but as a student in the fourth department, he was not one of Henry's students. George W. Carpenter was Herman's teacher. A marked improvement over Gorilla Arms, Carpenter, a civil engineer, was qualified to teach many different subjects.[45] Herman studied English grammar, penmanship, arithmetic and geography.

A previously neglected list of textbooks from the fourth department of Albany Academy when Herman was a student adds further information.[46] The listed textbooks include Warren Colburn's *Arithmetic*; Nathan Daboll's *Schoolmaster's Assistant*, best known as Daboll's *Arithmetic*; Jesse Olney's *Practical System of Modern Geography*; and William Woodbridge's *Rudiments of Geography*. Listing two mathematics and two geography textbooks, this inventory suggests that students in the fourth department worked at different levels according to their ability. Herman knew Olney's *Geography* and Daboll's *Arithmetic*.

Olney structured his geographical textbook as a series of questions and answers. Students were supposed to recite memorized answers when examined. 'For what is America distinguished?' Olney asked. The student was expected to reply, 'For its large rivers, numerous lakes, and its lofty and extended ranges of mountains.'[47] Olney's *Geography* would remain a classroom standard for the next three decades, though some questioned its pedagogical method. Recalling his childhood, one nineteenth-century educator quipped, 'We knew Olney's *Geography*, but were in blissful ignorance of geography.'[48]

Daboll's *Arithmetic* had developed such an authoritative reputation that the phrase 'according to Daboll' had become proverbial. Stubb mentions the book in *Moby-Dick*. Giving Stubb the same level of education he had received at Albany Academy, Melville implicitly ridiculed the school's curriculum. Stubb possesses just enough book learning to belittle others with even less.[49]

Ciphering books provided another way Herman learned arithmetic. Whereas Colburn's *Arithmetic* taught students their gazintas (2 gazinta 4 . . .), the ciphering book allowed them to perform more complex calculations. Mr Carpenter would dictate mathematical problems to the students, who transcribed them into their ciphering books. Each boy could then work at his own pace, letting the teacher see his answers once he was finished. Ciphering books let students show their work neatly and accurately.

With a blank notebook before them, many students doodled instead of doing their sums. Though Herman enjoyed drawing, he kept both pen and imagination in check while doing his. At the end of the school year, he had one of the neatest ciphering books in his class. In the last week of July the fourth department was examined in several subjects. Herman took first prize in ciphering books.[50]

Both Gansevoort and Herman began their second year at Albany Academy on 1 September 1831. Herman withdrew in mid-October. One theory says he contracted an illness that kept him from the classroom.[51] But that October was quite mild, delaying the cold and flu season. Besides, it seems unlikely that any illness could keep this burly youngster home sick. An alternate theory is that Allan Melvill's disastrous financial state caused Herman to leave school. Parents were supposed to pay tuition before each term began, but Herman's father typically went weeks into the semester before paying his children's tuition. By mid-October, unable to delay payment any longer, Allan Melvill found he could not afford tuition for both boys. He paid Gansevoort's tuition but took Herman from school, continuing the pattern of favouritism he had displayed throughout his second son's life. Consequently Herman was home to witness what occurred over the next few months.

Winter came swiftly. A deep snow fell on Sunday, 27 November 1831, deep enough for Albany citizens to hitch up their sleighs for the first time that season. The sound of sleigh bells augured in the Christmas holidays, but Allan Melvill, faced with enormous debts, had little to celebrate. Joseph Greenleaf, a Murray Street moneylender, had written from New York, urging him to repay his loans.[52] By Tuesday the 29th, Allan could no longer ignore this moneylender's requests. That day he left Albany for New York, where he met with Greenleaf, who showed him the financial claims against him. Allan took a few days to digest the information. He returned the papers to Greenleaf the following Wednesday before boarding the *Constellation* for Albany.[53]

With the establishment of the Hudson River Line the previous decade, steamboat travel between New York and Albany had become quite convenient. The fastest steamboats could make the trip in fifteen hours. The boat would depart New York at five in the afternoon, letting passengers enjoy drinks and dinner aboard ship before retiring to their berths. They would wake up in the morning, prepare their toilet and have breakfast. As they finished breakfast, ideally, the boat would pull into Albany.

Though the *Constellation* represented contemporary travel at its finest, it lacked one convenience associated with modern travel: a system of rapid communication. Since Morse's telegraph remained a year or two away, news between Albany and New York travelled only as fast as the fastest steamboat. When the *Constellation* pulled away from the dock in New York that Wednesday, the passengers and crew remained unaware that ice had closed the river at Albany, which usually remained open until late December.

The *Constellation* reached Poughkeepsie early on Thursday morning, but river ice prevented it from continuing north. Albany passengers had to fend for themselves in the freezing cold. After sunrise Allan hired an open wagon, which took him as far as Rhinebeck, where he spent Thursday night. The next morning he caught a ride in another open wagon. By dark Allan had only made it to the town of Hudson. He woke up Saturday morning to discover with some trepidation that the temperature had slipped below zero on the Fahrenheit scale. Allan managed to get a ride in a covered sleigh, which brought him to Greenbush at dusk. He was close to home but still had the river to cross. With no alternative, he walked across the Hudson on the ice, reaching home well after dark, exhausted and quite ill.[54]

Allan tried to tough out his illness, returning to the cap and fur store during the busiest time of the year. He should have been home in bed, but he had to do something to contribute to his family's support. The effort exacerbated his illness; he kept working into the first week of January, when he became too debilitated to leave the house. In a matter of days, according to his wife, Allan 'by reason of severe suffering was depriv'd of his Intellect'.[55] From his sick bed, he began to rave. Since Herman was not in school, he heard the sounds his father made and bore witness to the crumbling of his mind. Allan Melvill's raving would resurface in his son's writing: both Captain Ahab in *Moby-Dick* and Pierre Glendinning's father in *Pierre* display similar behaviour.

The fatiguing journey explains Allan's physical illness. The subfreezing temperatures and the arduous effort had lowered his body's defences. Perhaps he caught a cold that developed into pneumonia. His mental illness is more difficult to explain. In essence, he reached a point where his mind could no longer cope with reality. He had patterned his personal behaviour on what his conduct books told him, seeing himself as a proper gentleman, a successful businessman and the head of a happy household. Instead of doing what he most wanted to do – make his family happy – his reckless borrowing and spending had doomed them to financial disaster. When he recognized that his whole life had been a sham, it was too much to take. No longer could his mind reconcile image and reality.

Deranged and debilitated, Allan Melvill lingered two weeks further, but half an hour before midnight on Saturday, 28 January 1832, he passed away. The sorry task of sorting through Allan's belongings fell to his widow. When Maria came across his watch fob with a seal at its end, she presented it to their oldest son.[56] The watch fob symbolized that sixteen-year-old Gansevoort now had to take responsibility for the family. Allan Melvill's death ended Gansevoort's dreams of Harvard. Though worn at the waist, the watch fob sometimes felt like a chain around his neck. For Herman the memories of their father also hung heavy. *Redburn* recalls his happy childhood but then forces himself to stop: 'I must not think of those delightful days, before my father became a bankrupt, and died, and we removed from the city; for when I think of those days, something rises up in my throat and almost strangles me.'[57]

2

Work

The 'Cholera Summer' of 1832 left Albany a sad and lonely place. Those who could get out of town did. Those remaining burned pots of tar in the streets, a practice rooted in the folk belief that smoke could ward off disease. The burning tar and the summer sun covered the city with a patchwork of light and dark, forcing pedestrians like Herman Melville to pass through plumes of smoke on their way to work. While darkening the city and giving it a noxious smell, the smoke scarcely lessened the cholera. By 1 August, the day Herman turned thirteen, half a dozen people were dying in Albany from cholera every day.[1]

Herman was stuck in the city by himself. Believing desperate diseases required desperate measures, his mother had loaded all her boys and girls onto the Pittsfield stage at the first sign of cholera and brought them to the farm of Thomas and Mary Melvill. (Maria Melville added the final 'e' to the family name after her husband's death, but her in-laws remained Melvills.) Fleeing the cholera, she took Herman away from the bank clerk's job he had started some weeks earlier. As a mother her top priority was keeping her brood safe, dollars be damned. The day they reached Pittsfield Maria wrote to her brother Peter, urging him to flee. He reacted differently. Having secured the full-time job for his nephew, Peter insisted she send him back: Herman had responsibilities at the bank. Beholden to her brother, she acquiesced, putting her second son on the stage to Albany, a lamb sacrificed to Mammon.

Not until the following summer could Herman visit the farm on vacation. The open air was a welcome treat, and he could practically live on Aunt Mary's fresh milk, homemade bread and new butter.[2] His cousins were great fun, especially Julia, whose correspondence indicates her fondness for 'Herm'. With a good ear for conversation, Julia could write realistically when she wished but often told some stretchers. Sharp and sarcastic, she could match wits with Herm or Helen or whomever. Julia could be melancholy, but, like Herman, she dispelled the melancholy with self-effacing humour. Julia was close to Herm in both age and spirit.

The chance to run errands for his employer let Herman break the tedium of workaday Albany. When the bank sent him to Schenectady in March 1834, he took the train. The Mohawk and Hudson Railroad, one of America's first, began service between Albany and Schenectady in 1831. Drawn by a locomotive named DeWitt Clinton, the cars were little more than horse carriages hooked together and equipped with special wheels to fit the rails. The Albany–Schenectady route was a great convenience – or would be once railroads instituted regular timetables. Herman's experience shows that rail travel remained in a state of flux three years after service between the two cities began.

Entering the cap and fur business as manufacturer and retailer after their father's death, Gansevoort used the railway to transport merchandise but preferred travelling by horseback. On a business trip one afternoon that March Gansevoort rode to Schenectady. Upon entering the city astride his new horse, he stopped by Davis' Hotel, where he was shocked to see Herman, now fourteen, seated in the hotel bar. Gansevoort asked what he was doing there. Herman had not entered the hotel bar for a wee taste of the creature: he was stuck in Schenectady because there were no return trains that evening.[3]

Gansevoort suffered a crippling setback in May, when his factory burnt down. The fire forced him to rebuild his business.

He reduced the number of employees, hiring his brother to clerk in the retail store. This new job rescued Herman from the bank, but his work scarcely changed. Clerking in a store differed little from clerking in a bank. His animosity would surface in his writings. When the old lawyer in 'Bartleby, the Scrivener' asks Bartleby if he would like a clerkship in a dry-goods store, he replies, 'There is too much confinement about that. No, I would not like a clerkship.'[4]

The cap and fur store did have a sensual quality Herman enjoyed. Buffalo robes were one of Gansevoort's most profitable items. Herman loved their feel and smell and symbolism. Having teased his big brother when they were boys, Herman retained a playful streak. Something Ishmael says in *Moby-Dick* suggests that Herman used to shake a fresh buffalo robe while standing behind Gansevoort's horse to see how it would react. A young colt foaled in Vermont that has never encountered a buffalo, Ishmael explains in 'The Whiteness of the Whale', will smell its 'wild animal muskiness' when a fresh buffalo robe is shaken behind it. The colt will 'start, snort, and with bursting eyes paw the ground in phrensies of affright'.[5]

Both Gansevoort and Herman joined the Albany Young Men's Association for Mutual Improvement in the mid-1830s. Members gathered in its club rooms to read old books and discuss current events. The Melville brothers joined its debating society. Herman subsequently joined another debating club, the Philo Logos Society, serving as president. A controversial leader, Herman prolonged his disagreement with club members in the press. Filled with backbiting and personal invective, Herman's articles reflect his need for screed. It is disappointing that this small-minded newspaper controversy represents the first published work of the author of *Moby-Dick*.

Gansevoort had trouble keeping his business afloat during a nationwide depression. He filed for bankruptcy in April 1837, leaving Herman unemployed. Maria, who had sustained her oldest son's business by taking out loans on property she would inherit from her father's estate, convened a family council in June 1837 to determine the boys' future. Her third son Allan, now fourteen, would read law with Uncle Peter in Albany. Gansevoort would move to New York to read law. Uncle Thomas, who was planning to relocate to Galena, Illinois, before moving his family there, needed someone to run the Pittsfield farm that summer. The responsibility fell to seventeen-year-old Herman.[6] Besides reuniting him with Julia and other cousins, life there would put Herman in touch with the soil, letting him enjoy the outdoors and the life-giving forces the farm represented.

After he went to Pittsfield, Julia wrote to his sister Augusta, telling her it was great having Herm around. He was pleasant and always polite. Priscilla Melvill, an older cousin, called the Pittsfield farm Herman's first love.[7] A demanding mistress, the farm required much work, but it offered much in return, giving him woods and meadows and hillocks to explore. He familiarized himself with all its hidden spaces and high places. His favourite hunk of terrain was a huge rock from which he could overlook the countryside between the farm and the steeples of Pittsfield.

Reluctant to leave the area after finishing his summer work, Herman took a position at a district school near Pittsfield to teach the big-boned progeny of local farmers. He lasted a semester, returning to Albany shortly before his proud mother decided they could no longer stay in Albany and maintain their lifestyle. They would move 9 miles (14 km) north to Lansingburgh, where the cost of living was lower.

Herman next sought a position on the Erie Canal. Since it opened in 1825, the canal had outgrown itself. It carried so many emigrants and so much cargo westward it needed to be widened and deepened significantly. Being a civil engineer on the Erie Canal offered a more productive way to put his mathematical skills to work than being a bank clerk. Civil engineering involved both mental and physical labour; canal work would let him contribute to the development of the nation, helping give people an efficient way west.

The Lansingburgh Academy offered a suitable surveying and engineering course. After a review of arithmetic, Herman studied the principles of measurement, learning how to ascertain lengths, areas and volumes. Instruction in surveying took him out of the classroom and into nearby fields, where he practised the use of chain, compass and theodolite. He also learned enough trigonometry to calculate heights and distances.[8] Herman successfully completed the course in the first week of April 1839 but never secured the position he sought. He could have found similar work on the railroad, but railways lacked the appeal waterways had for Melville. Once the canal job fell through, he devoted little further effort towards a career in civil engineering.

Herman amused himself in Lansingburgh with some newspaper sketches, 'Fragments from a Writing Desk'. For Fragment No. 1 he assumed the persona of a protégé writing to his mentor. The letter writer imagines his correspondent seated on a comfy sofa holding a 'huge-clasped quarto' in his lap with his legs flung across the back of a 'straight limbed, stiff-necked, quaint old chair', which, as a mutual friend facetiously asserted, 'was the identical seat in which old Burton composed his *Anatomy of Melancholy*'.[9] Fragment No. 1 demonstrates Melville's sense of ease, his narrative aplomb. The article also reflects his grasp of the material culture: he provides sufficient detail for readers to feel the softness of the sofa, see the quaintness of the chair and wonder what secrets lie within that clasped quarto. The reference to Burton's *Anatomy of Melancholy* reveals Melville's awareness of this classic of whimsy and erudition. He had yet to read it, the evidence suggests, but knew this bookish reference would enhance his article's atmosphere. The reference also emphasizes the friends' camaraderie. They possess sufficient literary knowledge to get a joke about a centuries-old book.

With no work on land, Herman went to New York, where, on 5 June 1839, he sailed as a green hand aboard the *St Lawrence*, a copper-bottomed, copper-fastened ship carrying cotton to Liverpool.[10] Melville underwent the trials and tribulations all green hands undergo their first time at sea. *Redburn* approximates its author's initiation into the foremastman's world. His fellow sailors tormented Melville, forcing him to perform arduous and irksome chores. He learned about life in the forecastle, the cramped space in the front of the ship – before the mast – where the common sailors slept and talked and belched and farted. Melville came to know the lore of the sailor, the sayings, superstitions, customs and conventions, all of which helped him understand what to do aboard ship and what not to do. He also learned how to scramble up the rigging and down in fair weather and foul and how to reef a sail while balancing precariously one hundred feet above the deck of the ship.

In July the *St Lawrence* entered Prince's Dock, the largest in Liverpool, where it would stay for weeks. Melville had light duties to perform, but, like Redburn, he had time to explore the city. He was always attracted to warm, cosy spaces, 'snuggeries', he called them. The cabin of a local vessel known as a salt drogher, according to *Redburn*, was

> the prettiest, charmingest, most delightful little dog-hole
> in the world; not much bigger than an old fashioned
> alcove for a bed. It is lighted by little round glasses placed
> in the deck; so that to the insider, the ceiling is like a
> small firmament twinkling with astral radiations.[11]

One Irish newspaper editor enjoyed his description of the salt drogher so much he reprinted it. Clearly Melville was not the only one attracted to snug little spaces that could make one room an everywhere.[12]

Home from Liverpool, Melville again found himself unemployed and looking for work. He secured a teaching position at an academy in Greenbush, New York. Unable to pay its bills or its teachers, the academy closed in May 1840. Melville's inability to find gainful employment was frustrating. His friend Eli Fly had been reading law with Herman's Uncle Peter, but he also longed for a change. Together they devised a solution: go west.

Melville later spoke of being 'a vagabond' along the Erie Canal; he and Fly most likely crossed New York using a combination of Shanks's mare and canal boat, riding whenever a friendly boatman let them leave the towpath and hop aboard a freighter. In 'The *Town-Ho*'s Story' Ishmael conveys his appreciation for a good turn done him by a canal boatman with 'as stiff an arm to back a poor stranger in a strait, as to plunder a wealthy one'.[13]

At Buffalo Melville and Fly could board a steamboat for the first leg of the thousand-mile journey through the Great Lakes. Neither recorded their precise route, but brief comments scattered across Melville's writings outline their American odyssey. Steamboats from Buffalo to Detroit were filled with westbound emigrants and their wagons, oxen and household gods. The Lake Erie steamboat stopped at Cleveland long enough to let them explore the city. Redburn's friend Harry Bolton has a similar experience in Liverpool, where 'he was as much in a foreign land, as if he were already on the shores of Lake Erie; so that he strolled about . . . in perfect abandonment.'[14] Hundreds of miles west of home, Melville enjoyed a great sense of freedom. He could wander about Cleveland doing whatever he wished. He knew no one. There was nobody to censure his behaviour, to tell him what to do or what not to do. The anonymity was exhilarating.

Amazed by the sheer size of Lake Erie, Melville would use it as a fanciful metaphor, a hyperbolic unit of measurement. In *Mardi* he mentions a fat uncle with a big paunch and imagines him consuming many 'droves of oxen and Lake Eries of wine'.[15] The route from Sandusky to Detroit offered a fine view of Lake Erie's southwestern coastline:

> The beautiful and curving shores of the main land, and of the insular territories, covered as they generally are with unbroken forests, and opening channels and bays in every direction, lend a vision of enchantment, rarely equalled.[16]

After the calm and beauty of southwestern Lake Erie, Detroit startled disembarking passengers. As steamships approached, hotelkeepers swarmed the docks, each proclaiming his establishment to be the best. North from Detroit the Chicago boat steamed past Belle Isle and crossed Lake St Clair, which was like 'flying from a world, violated by the track and by the hand of man, into a world of virgin waters and into a virgin wilderness'.[17] Passengers could tour Fort Gratiot before entering Lake Huron. They also stopped at Fort Mackinac. In 'The *Town-Ho*'s Story' Ishmael mentions 'the goat-like craggy guns of lofty Mackinaw'. Melville also incorporated imagery from this trip in *Mardi*, describing how 'a mighty moose swam stately as a seventy-four, and backward tossed his antlered wilderness in the air.' Melville and Fly sailed the length of Lake Michigan to Chicago, from which they travelled overland almost as far as the Mississippi River.[18]

In Galena Melville was reunited with Uncle Thomas, Aunt Mary and his Melvill cousins. They could scarcely mask their poverty, but amid the dark squalor Melville could spy a beacon of the glowing past: that legendary vial of tea from the Boston Tea Party.[19] Galena itself offered few opportunities for young men seeking professional careers. Their quest for employment failed; their journey never became anything more than a low-budget sightseeing trip.

The whaling voyage he would soon undertake would be the most important journey of Melville's life; his inland excursion may be the second most important. Delving into the heart of America before seeing the South Pacific, he could compare locales and recognize what his national geography represented. In Melville's work the Great Lakes stand for the greatness of America; the prairie represents the continent's natural fecundity; and the Mississippi symbolizes the political, social and moral complexities facing the nation.[20]

Melville's return to New York from the West coincided with the year's biggest publishing event: the release of *Two Years before the Mast*, a personal narrative of ocean-going adventure by Richard Henry Dana Jr, which Melville read with sympathy and affection.[21] Dana presented an alternate way of writing about the sea. Eschewing Romantic adventure for matter-of-fact detail, *Two Years before the Mast* possesses a realism absent from earlier nineteenth-century literature. Dana's book, Melville observed, 'impairs the relish with which we read Byron's spiritual address to the ocean'. Melville's comparison deflates Byron's youthful associations and undermines his Romantic imagery:

> When the noble poet raves about laying his hands upon
> the ocean's mane (in other words manipulating the
> crest of a wave) the most vivid image suggested is that
> of a valetudinarian bather at Rockaway, spluttering and
> choking in the surf, with his mouth full of brine.[22]

Roaming the streets of Manhattan looking for work, Melville found himself returning to the wharves, where shipping agencies that sought would-be sailors posted notices whenever they needed men. In *Etchings of a Whaling Cruise* J. Ross Browne describes the shipping agents. Reviewing Browne, Melville supplied additional information from personal experience, facetiously describing the misleading placards outside their offices that made it seem as though the agents performed a public service by finding employment for able-bodied men. Melville clarified this

J. Ross Browne, wood engraving, 1868.

misconception: 'The agent's business, be it understood, consists in decoying "green hands" to send on to the different whaling ports.'[23] 'Whaling, gentlemen, is tolerably hard at first, but it's the finest business in the world for enterprising young men,' an agent told Browne and his friend. 'There's nothing like it. You can see the world; you can see something of life!'

In late December Herman and Gansevoort went to Fairhaven, where several whalers were preparing to sail, including a brand-new vessel, the *Acushnet*. On Christmas Day Herman signed on as a green hand, receiving a 1/175th lay, the fraction of the total profit he would receive at the voyage's end. An ocean voyage whose duration was counted in years was daunting, but Herman took comfort in it. Aboard the *Acushnet* he would not have to worry about where his next sixpence was coming from, nor would he have to bother looking, applying or interviewing for any other job.

Seaman's Bethel, West Side of Johnny Cake Hill (formerly Bethel Street),
New Bedford, Bristol County, Massachusetts, 1961.

Gansevoort said he had never seen his brother 'so completely
happy, as when he had determined upon a situation and all was
settled'.[24]

On Sunday, the 27th, Gansevoort and Herman attended services
together at the Seaman's Bethel in New Bedford. The Reverend
Enoch Mudge delivered a sermon that would influence the one
Father Mapple delivers in *Moby-Dick*, though the lyricism of
Mapple's sermon makes it sound more like the homilies Jeremy
Taylor delivered at Golden Grove. Before Gansevoort said goodbye

to his brother, they went shopping. Herman traded his overcoat and some additional items of shore toggery for the rugged wear – stout duck trousers, red flannel shirt, heavy Havre frock – he would need aboard the *Acushnet*.[25]

The *Acushnet* set sail on 3 January 1841. The captain typically summoned the crew to welcome them aboard and warn them to obey orders. There was no set time for this traditional speech. In *Moby-Dick* Melville would delay Captain Ahab's speech to enhance the story's mystery. In *Two Years before the Mast* the mates divide the crew into watches just before their captain gives 'a short characteristic speech, walking the quarter-deck with a cigar in his mouth, and dropping the words out between the puffs'.[26] In *Etchings of a Whaling Cruise* the captain delivers his characteristic speech after disciplining a troublesome hand. The speech thus becomes a matter of laying down the law.

Presumably following tradition, Captain Valentine Pease Jr, master of the *Acushnet*, called his men aft around the time they had selected their watches, which resembled how schoolboys chose teams for prisoners' base. Forty-three years old, Pease was quite tall, according to a nephew. He wore side whiskers and an imperial, a small, pointed beard beneath his lower lip. Otherwise he resembled any other whaling captain. When asked if Captain Vangs, the hard-hearted skipper in *Typee*, resembled his uncle, the nephew replied, 'No, I don't recall that Uncle Val was a harsh man . . . I should say he was an upright man, but at times quite profane.'[27] The nephew's opinion was based on Captain Pease's behaviour ashore, which did not necessarily reflect his behaviour at sea. After sailing aboard the *Acushnet*, Melville remarked, 'The god Janus never had two more decidedly different faces than your sea captain.'[28]

'I suppose you all know what you came a whaling for? If you don't, I'll tell you. You came to make a voyage, and I intend you shall make one. You didn't come to play; no, you came for oil; you came to work.' These are the words the captain speaks as he addresses the men in *Etchings of a Whaling Cruise,* but they approximate what Captain Pease said to the crew of the *Acushnet.* Whereas Browne's captain takes a step or two on the quarter deck between sentences, Captain Pease, perhaps, gave his imperial a twist during the pauses in his speech.

'We didn't ship you to be idle here. No, no, that ain't what we shipped you for, by a grand sight. If you think it is, you'll find yourselves mistaken', Browne's captain says. 'Now, the sooner you get a cargo of oil, the sooner you'll get home.'[29]

Little is known about the 69-day passage of the *Acushnet* from Fairhaven to Rio de Janeiro save for one telling detail: it entered the harbour at Rio laden with 150 barrels of sperm oil.[30] Since sperm whales yield around sixty barrels of oil, the crew spotted, hunted, killed and tried out two or three whales before Rio. The whole process that Melville would describe in long and loving detail in *Moby-Dick*, everything from the first lowering to stowing down and clearing up, he learned in the Atlantic, not the Pacific. Despite his book's extraordinary detail, sometimes it is difficult to separate the fact from the fat. How did Melville feel when he first hunted for whales on the way to Rio?

Before he wrote *Moby-Dick*, Melville recorded much about his personal whaling experience in his review of Browne's *Etchings*, including what happened once the harpooneer darted his harpoon:

It flies from his hands – and where are we then, my lovelies? – It's all a mist, a crash, – a horrible blending of sounds and sights, as the agonized whale lashes the water around him into suds and vapor – dashes the boat aside, and at last rushes, madly, through the water towing after him the half-filled craft which rocks from side to side while the disordered crew, clutch at the gunwale to avoid being tossed out. Meanwhile all sorts of horrific edged tools – lances, harpoons and spades – are slipping about; and the imminent line itself – smoking round

the logger-head and passing along the entire length of the
boat – is almost death to handle, though it grazes your person.
    But all this is nothing to what follows. As yet you have but
simply *fastened* to the whale: he must be fought and killed.
But let imagination supply the rest: – the monster staving the
boat with a single sweep of his ponderous flukes; – taking its
bows between his jaws (as is frequently the case) and playing
with it, as a cat with a mouse. Sometimes he bites it in twain;
sometimes crunches it into chips, and strews the sea with them.[31]

As Captain Pease plotted his course after Rio, the *Acushnet* sailed
between the Falklands and the southern coast of Patagonia on its
way towards Cape Horn. Rounding the cape took on the quality of
a mythic journey to the underworld for Melville. In *White-Jacket* he
asks: 'Was the descent of Orpheus, Ulysses, or Dante into Hell, one
whit more hardy and sublime than the first navigator's weathering
of that terrible Cape?'[32] Having safely rounded Cape Horn, Melville
entered the Pacific, something he had dreamed of doing all his life.
The chapter in *Moby-Dick* on the subject is the greatest paean to the
Pacific in American literature.
    Though whalemen worked hard, they made time for fun.
The gam, a pleasurable encounter between two ships, let them
socialize at sea. In August 1841 the *Acushnet* enjoyed a three-day
gam with the *Lima*, a Nantucket whaler, during which Melville
met William Henry Chase, the son of Owen Chase, who had
written the grim and gruesome *Narrative of the Most Extraordinary
and Distressing Shipwreck of the Whale-ship Essex*. William Chase
loaned a copy to Melville, who would recall, 'The reading of
this wondrous story upon the landless sea, and close to the very
latitude of the shipwreck had a surprising effect upon me.'[33] Once
the *Essex* was stove by a whale and sunk, its men were forced into
open boats a thousand miles from land to endure starvation-
induced cannibalism.

The foreground of this Currier and Ives lithograph, *Whale Fishery: Attacking a Right Whale*, c. 1856, depicts a right whale. The background may be more interesting: it provides a good illustration of whalemen unfurling the length of whale flesh known as 'the blanket'.

Richard Tobias Greene, the crew member Melville would immortalize as Toby in *Typee*, was an intelligent, sensitive man. At 21 he was the same age as Melville. At five feet, five and a half inches tall he looked up to Melville, who is listed as five feet, nine and a half.[34] Independent testimony confirms Melville's portrayal. One acquaintance characterized Greene as modest and unassuming. Another found him 'whole-hearted, genial, companionable' and 'full of frankness, amiability, and jollity'. During their 'pleasant moonlight watches', the two became close a s they whiled away the hours 'with yarn and song'.[35]

Another member of their watch supplied fun of a different sort. With a mug 'as rough as a Macadamized road', he went by the nickname 'Jack Nastyface'. Greene's favourite Jack Nastyface anecdote dates from when the *Acushnet* crossed the equator with Jack at the masthead.[36] Once his shift ended, he descended to the deck. His shipmates informed him they had crossed the equator while he was aloft.

'The devil we did!' Jack exclaimed.

The model for Archy in *Moby-Dick*, Jack Nastyface is the kind of sailor who has to be the first to know the latest news. Archy says he already knew about Fedallah and his men before they appeared on deck. Jack Nastyface behaved similarly. After being told about the equatorial crossing, he quickly recovered his composure and told the others he already knew they had crossed the line. 'Can't ye tell us some news?' he asked. 'Didn't I see it as well as you did, and better too? Wasn't I aloft? I saw the line before any man aboard.'

The fourth week of June 1842 the *Acushnet* neared Nukahiva, an island in the Marquesas. The island's beauty astonished them, but its scenery provided only part of the allure. For sailors who had seen little else but whales and water and one another for several months, Nukahiva had a more attractive feature. As the *Acushnet* anchored in Taiohae Bay, naked island girls swam out to meet them. Tommo – Melville's fictional counterpart in *Typee* – exclaimed, 'What a sight for us bachelor sailors! how avoid so dire a temptation?' Many could not. Though Melville romanticized his experience in *Typee*, his portrayal of what happened upon the ship's arrival sounds like realism: 'Our ship was now wholly given up to every species of riot and debauchery. Not the feeblest barrier was interposed between the unholy passions of the crew and their unlimited gratification.'[37] Melville portrayed Tommo as a healthy, upright young man who would not dare indulge in such debauchery, but there is no telling whether the character's behaviour reflects his creator's. One poetic admirer has Melville leaping ashore 'to greet with kisses / The dainty, dimpled nutbrown misses'.[38]

As the island girls climbed aboard the *Acushnet* that June, Herman's family had no idea what he was doing. That month

Gansevoort read a magazine article about an American whaler in the South Pacific during a violent storm, which let him imagine his brother's adventures.[39] 'We hear quite accidentally that Herman was gone to sea,' Julia wrote Augusta that same month. 'I was cut out for an old maid.'[40] Comparing her situation with Herm's, Julia sadly understood the limits to her life. Whereas Herman could sail wherever he wished, she was stuck wherever her family settled. All the popular American rhetoric about going west to succeed had never applied to girls. Julia faced the same situation in Galena she had faced in Pittsfield, marriage or death being the only ways out from under her father's roof. Uncle Thomas's inability to provide Julia with a dowry made it unlikely that she would marry, despite her spunk.

Though Melville's experience on Nukahiva would inspire *Typee*, the book must not be read as autobiography, no matter how tempting. After *Typee* appeared Greene published a newspaper article structured as a letter to Melville.[41] Greene's, the only other account of their time in Typee Valley, is not exactly unvarnished truth. Confirming what his friend had written, Greene refuted Melville's critics, making himself complicit in his fiction.

Taken together, the similarities between Melville's version and Greene's approximate the truth. Both depict their challenging trek through Nukahiva's craggy wilderness. Greene's account mentions Melville's lameness twice, suggesting that Tommo's lameness in *Typee* is based on fact. Greene also uses some of the same names as *Typee*, including Marheyo – the islander Tommo and Toby live with – and Mow-Mow, who had only one eye, according to both Melville and Greene. The most memorable character in *Typee*, of course, is Fayaway, the beautiful native girl who enchants Tommo. Greene verifies her existence, implying that she and Melville formed some kind of romantic attachment. Melville left Nukahiva after less than one month, not four, as *Typee* has it. And his escape was not the climax of a thrilling chase: the Typee natives simply traded him for some trinkets offered by Captain Henry Ventom, the skipper of the *Lucy Ann*, a Sydney whaler.

Omoo, the sequel to *Typee*, presents a fictionalized version of the *Lucy Ann*'s voyage. Though *Omoo* resumes Melville's story where *Typee* leaves off, it should not be read as autobiography either. In the case of *Omoo* numerous supporting documents survive to chronicle the voyage. The crew list reveals much. The man who would be Doctor Long Ghost in *Omoo*, for example, signed aboard the *Lucy Ann* in Sydney as 'John B. Troy'. Melville's name appears with those of other sailors recruited in the Marquesas. The *Lucy Ann* resumed whaling beyond the Marquesas, but once illness struck down Captain Ventom, the first mate sailed the ship to Tahiti.[42]

At Papeete the rebellious crew refused to obey any more orders. The most recalcitrant crew members, including Troy but not Melville, were manacled and taken to the brig of a French warship. Before leaving Tahiti, the French admiral ordered them ashore into the custody of the British consul, who turned them over to the local constable. Confined by night in a makeshift calaboose, the prisoners could roam the island by day. Before September 1842 ended, Melville, too, refused to obey orders and joined the other prisoners. His behaviour seems quite shrewd in retrospect. When faced with the possibility of being manacled in the brig of a French warship, he obeyed orders, but when the opportunity of being left on land in an open-air confinement arose, he suddenly refused to obey.[43]

After the *Lucy Ann* left Tahiti on 15 October 1842, the supervision of its disobedient men lessened, and they gradually walked away from the calaboose. Melville and Troy briefly became fieldhands at a potato farm on Eimeo but soon left to explore other parts of that island.[44] The *Charles and Henry*, a Nantucket whaler, took Melville from Eimeo the first week of November 1842.

The six months Melville spent aboard the *Charles and Henry* were largely uneventful. When it reached Maui on 27 April 1843, he left the ship to linger in the Sandwich Islands. After exploring Maui he went to Oahu. Honolulu was developing rapidly. Here's one indication: the city now had seven bowling alleys.[45] The popularity of bowling in Honolulu let Melville find work as a pinsetter. In his spare time he became an excellent bowler. Attracting both sensitive souls and ne'er-do-wells, the bowling alley is a paradoxical place where the sound of tumbling pins induces a mood of quiet contemplation. Hawaii also exposed Melville to a different recreational pursuit: surfing. There is no evidence that he attempted to surf, but Melville did spend time at Waikiki watching the young Hawaiian men. He would incorporate a lively description of surfing in *Mardi*.[46]

Thinking he could live in Honolulu indefinitely, Melville sought a more stable position. His previous experience as a clerk created an opportunity. One day Melville met an English entrepreneur who took a shine to him and offered him a position as clerk and bookkeeper of his new Honolulu dry goods store. For the time being Melville's future seemed set.[47]

On 3 August 1843, two days after Melville turned 24, the *United States*, the flagship of the American Pacific Squadron, reached Honolulu. Birthdays were reflective times for Melville. The arrival of the *United States* coincided with a bout of homesickness. Always impulsive, Melville quit the dry goods store and joined the navy. He signed up as an ordinary seaman for three years or the cruise, whichever came first.

From Honolulu the ship took a big loop around the South Pacific, giving Melville a retrospective view of his travels. Having already spent a month in the Marquesas, Melville could amuse his new shipmates with stories about his intimacy with the natives. The *United States* stopped at Nukahiva and Tahiti before heading east to Valparaíso, which it reached the first week of December 1843. Built on 'cindery, earthquaky hills', Valparaíso, as Robert Tomes noticed upon visiting the city, seemed ready to slip into the sea.[48] The *United States* next headed to Callao, remaining there almost interminably. Melville spent countless hours gazing into the depths of the bay. He would ask the readers of *Mardi*: 'Saw you ever the hillocks of old Spanish anchors, and anchor-stocks of ancient galleons, at the bottom of Callao Bay?'[49] Besides staring into the depths of the bay, Melville studied the coast. Lima was visible in the distance. The setting sun displayed it best.

One day Melville received shore leave. Enjoying the freedom, he walked from Callao to Lima, seeing 'herds of panniered mules, driven . . . by mounted Indians, along the great road from Callao to Lima'.[50] He would incorporate a description of the city in 'The Whiteness of the Whale':

> Lima has taken the white veil; and there is a higher horror in this whiteness of her woe. Old as Pizarro, this whiteness keeps her ruins for ever new; admits not the cheerful green-ness of complete decay; spreads over her broken ramparts the rigid pallor of an apoplexy that fixes its own distortions.[51]

The *United States* sailed north to Mazatlán before returning to Callao, where it lingered until after the Fourth of July 1844. Three more months and another perilous trip around Cape Horn would find Melville in Boston honourably discharged from the navy and wondering where life would take him next.

3

The New Robinson Crusoe

Back in Lansingburgh by Halloween, Melville received a warm family welcome. His sisters peppered him with questions, wanting to know where he had gone and what he had done. Having honed his natural storytelling abilities during long, dark nights in the forecastle, he enchanted them with an almost endless stream of stories. According to a friend, Herman's adventures 'beguiled the long winter hours of his own home circle'.[1]

'Why don't you put in book form that story of your South Sea adventures which we all enjoy so much?' one family member asked.

Richard Henry Dana Jr had established his literary reputation with *Two Years before the Mast*. Melville knew his own odyssey was more exotic and action-packed. Though intrigued with the possibility, he understood how difficult it would be to make a living with his pen. Literature sometimes offered a path to preferment in antebellum America. Perhaps he could sustain a writing career long enough to establish a personal reputation leading to permanent employment. Never one to linger over a decision, Melville quickly made up his mind: he would become a writer.

Drafting the story of his far-flung experiences, Melville chose a persona close but not identical to himself. Tommo, as he named his fictional persona, let Melville veer from the truth to enhance his narrative. *Typee* begins aboard the *Acushnet*, which Melville renamed the *Dolly*. Once they reach Nukahiva, Tommo and Toby get shore leave and disappear into the bush. They climb a series of wet and wooded ridges before descending into a lush valley, afraid it may belong to the supposedly cannibalistic Typee.

Typee Valley hardly resembles a land of cannibals. The fertile valley seems like paradise, a place of joy and rejuvenation where the natives welcome them with friendship; where necessary sustenance grows within easy reach, no cultivation required; where civilization in the form of proselytizing Christian missionaries has yet to penetrate; where people walk around naked, or nearly so, their skin forming a canvas for local tattoo artists to practise their craft; where swimming with naked girls will form a major pastime for Tommo; and where a nymphet named Fayaway will steal his heart. It is also a place where Tommo and Toby are entrapped. Theirs is a pleasant confinement but a confinement nonetheless.

Having suffered a serious injury that makes walking painful, Tommo must be toted around by his manservant and gaoler, Kory-Kory. Toby successfully escapes but never returns to rescue Tommo. Tommo admits: 'No tidings of Toby ever reached me; he had gone never to return.'[2] Though *Typee* exaggerates Melville's personal adventures, the part about Toby never returning is true. Tommo's admission lessens the suspense: no longer do we anticipate Toby's surprise reappearance. But Melville does create some mystery. What happened to Toby? What kind of terrible trouble could have prevented him from rescuing his friend?

Toby's departure gives Tommo and Fayaway more time together, but his absence lessens the drama and the humour. The chapters that follow Toby's escape draw heavily from other travel narratives to supply information about the habits and lifestyle of the Typee natives. The 31st chapter marks a major shift. Though it continues to relate various aspects of Typee culture, it does so in a different manner. Instead of being devoted to a single topic, like some previous chapters, it consists of several brief sections treating a variety of topics, each separated from the next by a row of asterisks. Melville's technique in this chapter anticipates the cinematic montage, in which several brief shots are joined together to form a sequence that compresses space, time and information. Through similar compression, Melville accelerates the action of the story, propelling readers toward the drama of the final chapters.

The last chapter, which relates Tommo's thrilling escape from Nukahiva, shows that by the end of his first book Melville had mastered the dramatic possibilities of the chase. The penultimate chapter, in contrast, is contemplative. Taking an understated tone, Melville makes the composition of *Typee* part of the story. The chapter's conclusion depicts Tommo as he writes his personal narrative in a modern city, presumably New York, where Melville wrote much of *Typee* at his brothers' Wall Street law office. Tommo's memory of the pi-pi – the veranda of the dwelling where he lived – induces personal reflection:

> Just beyond the pi-pi, and disposed in a triangle before the entrance of the house, were three magnificent bread-fruit trees. At this moment I can recall to my mind their slender shafts, and the graceful inequalities of their bark, on which my eye was accustomed to dwell day after day in the midst of my solitary musings. It is strange how inanimate objects will twine themselves into our affections, especially in the hour of affliction. Even now, amidst all the bustle and stir of the proud and busy city in which I am dwelling, the image of those three trees seems to come as vividly before my eyes as if they were actually present, and I still feel the soothing quiet pleasure which I then had in watching hour after hour their topmost boughs waving gracefully in the breeze.[3]

In Tommo's memory Typee Valley has become what A. E. Housman calls a 'land of lost content', a magical world, a place of simplicity and sweetness to which he can never return. With this beautiful yet melancholy paragraph, with its contrast between his current self and his earlier one, now and then, here and elsewhere, Melville manipulates memory, place and time, foreshadowing a direction his writing would take as it matured.

Melville entered his brothers' Manhattan circle of lawyerly and literary friends. 'There is no place like a law-office for making a fashionable acquaintance,' Richard Grant White observed.[4] The friends they made in the neighbourhood included a gifted writer and newspaper editor named Charles Fenno Hoffman. In his boyhood Hoffman had been maimed while playing around the Cortland Street Dock. A literary man with a wooden leg, Hoffman did not let physical debility slow him down. He had taken an extended tour of the West on horseback in the 1830s, travelling as far as Missouri. He published his travels as *A Winter in the West*, a work Melville would echo in *The Confidence-Man*. Hoffman expressed an interest in *Typee*, so Gansevoort Melville kept him apprised of its status, knowing a friendly notice in his newspaper would boost sales.[5]

Once he had finished *Typee*, Melville submitted the manuscript to the Harpers. Frederick Saunders, their English-born literary advisor, read it with excitement. His report was unequivocal: 'This work if not as good as *Robinson Crusoe*, seems to me to be not far behind it.'[6] The Harper brothers did not base their decision solely on his report. They rejected *Typee* because 'it was impossible that it could be true and therefore was without real value.'[7] The Harpers' rejection reflects the ongoing bias against fiction, which many readers still considered unworthy of serious literary attention.

Melville did not take the rejection well, seeing it as a rejection of his entire approach to writing. Unsure what to do next, he left the manuscript at his brothers' office, where their journalist friend Thomas Low Nichols read it. On Nichols's advice Gansevoort took it to London once he was appointed secretary of the U.S. legation, an appointment rewarding his service as a stump speaker during James K. Polk's successful presidential campaign.[8]

John Sartain, *Charles Fenno Hoffman*, 19th-century engraving.

Gansevoort offered *Typee* to John Murray, one of London's most prestigious publishers. Murray made non-fiction his niche: biography, history, memoirs and travel. The Copyright Act that Parliament passed in 1842, which bolstered provisions against foreign piracy, provided the impetus for Murray's Colonial and Home Library, the first series of British books published for the colonies. Parliament could do nothing to prevent American publishers from pirating British books, but it could make illegal the importation of u.s. piracies into the British Empire. The legislative provisions were designed to open the colonial market to British publishers, especially Canada, which was overrun with pirated reprints from the USA. Colonial sales proved disappointing. The new legislation did little to stop the influx of pirated reprints into Canada. Home sales helped sustain the series. Less than a year after its start, Murray transposed the series title to reflect its shift in emphasis. The Colonial and Home Library became the Home and Colonial Library.[9]

After receiving a portion of the *Typee* manuscript, Murray wrote to Gansevoort Melville with his thoughts. He appreciated its narrative drama and racy style, but 'scented the forbidden thing – the taint of fiction'.[10] Murray wondered whether the author and the protagonist were two different people. He did not reject the manuscript outright but asked Gansevoort to submit the rest. Gansevoort did, assuring him that author and adventurer were the same.

In the first week of November 1845 Gansevoort wrote to Herman to express his confidence in *Typee*'s success. Though eager to get the work to press, Gansevoort learned that Herman had written more material at the last minute, a pattern of behaviour he would repeat throughout his career. The first week of December Gansevoort received the late insertions and sent them to Murray. In his cover letter he explained that the supplemental text would alleviate Murray's uncertainties, giving the work more realism and helping to convince readers of its veracity.

Murray handed the manuscript to Henry Milton. What Saunders was to the Harpers, Milton was to Murray, a reader who provided advice regarding a work's quality. Milton also edited manuscripts to make them suitable for publication. Working on a piecemeal basis, he billed Murray a total of 24 hours to read *Typee*. The time indicates that Milton read the manuscript carefully and conscientiously. Once Milton finished reading it, Murray accepted *Typee* for publication and offered an outright sum of £100. Gansevoort accepted. With an agreement in place Murray

John Sartain, *Washington Irving*, after Gilbert Stuart Newton, 19th-century engraving.

let Milton edit the manuscript for publication. Milton spent a total of 168 and a half hours revising *Typee*, earning over £50 for his work, more than half what Melville received.[11]

Once the Murray edition was in page proofs, Washington Irving happened to stop by the American legation. He befriended Gansevoort, who showed him the *Typee* proofsheets. Irving found Herman's prose exquisite and offered to help place *Typee* with an American publisher. He walked Gansevoort to Wiley and Putnam's

London office to introduce him to George Palmer Putnam, who oversaw the firm's British and Continental operations. Gansevoort lent him the proofsheets on a Saturday night. Putnam enjoyed them so much he skipped church Sunday morning to read *Typee*. He, too, found it reminiscent of *Robinson Crusoe* and accepted *Typee* for publication.[12]

'It looks well – God speed it': so wrote Gansevoort in his journal in late February 1846 upon receiving his first copy of *Typee* or, as Murray titled the British edition, *Narrative of a Four Months' Residence among the Natives of a Valley of the Marquesas Islands; or, A Peep at Polynesian Life*. Herman hated Murray's verbose title. Instead of the author's catchy, if cryptic, two-syllable title, Murray coined a wordy title laden with prepositions. The book became known among British readers as *Marquesas Islands*.

As Murray predicted, many readers questioned the book's veracity, finding *Marquesas Islands* too well written for a foremastman. Some accepted it at face value. *The Magnet*, one of the earliest London newspapers to review *Marquesas Islands*, identified Melville as an American traveller whose fondness for adventure had tempted him beyond the bounds of prudence. Given the high quality of Melville's prose, the *Hampshire Advertiser* found him a 'well-educated young man' and naturally assumed he was an officer.[13]

The review in *The Era*, the latest to appear in the dailies, summarizes the critical reception of *Marquesas Islands*. Those readers who had taken the book for truth puzzled the reviewer:

> Although *The Marquesas Islands* is not all that sundry enraptured critics have made it out to be, it may bear comparison with any work of fiction our own press has recently produced; for a work of fiction it indisputably is. How any of our contemporaries could persuade themselves that they were reading fact is astonishing.

To accept its fictional quality was the best way to appreciate the book, according to *The Era*. It saved readers from questioning every little detail and let them enjoy 'the glow and warmth of the whole'.[14]

The British annuals also noticed *Marquesas Islands. The Recreation: A Gift-book for Young Readers*, John Menzies's collection of adventure stories extracted from recent travel writings, contains a 24-page selection from *Marquesas Islands*. Menzies chose the most action-packed episodes, devoting the greatest space to Melville's flight with Toby through the rugged wilderness and his final escape. 'Escape from the Island', the frontispiece to *The Recreation*, illustrates a dramatic moment from *Marquesas Islands*. Engraver J. R. Jobbins had no idea what Melville really looked like, but that didn't stop his imagination.

In 'Escape from the Island' Melville stands on the beach consoling the broken-hearted (and topless) Fayaway, who holds his hand and rests her head on his shoulder. Behind Melville stand Marheyo and Kory-Kory. Bald, bearded and wearing togas, the two look more like Roman statesmen than South Pacific islanders. In the foreground, Karakoee, whom Melville describes as an Oahu Kannaka, stands in the surf confronting the sword-wielding Mow-Mow, muscular and ferocious. In the boat, two men row and a third holds a pole to steer and steady the vessel. Though Melville called them islanders, Jobbins depicted them in Eastern garb: turbans, tunics and earrings. Jobbins took many liberties with Melville's story, but his illustration shows how *Typee* fired the minds of its readers, prompting them to imagine all sorts of exotic details from Melville's South Pacific.

Published in New York by Wiley and Putnam the month after *Marquesas Islands*, *Typee* was greeted enthusiastically. Charles Fenno Hoffman found it 'one of the most delightful and well written narratives that ever came from an American pen'. He linked *Typee* with some famous works of British literature, calling Melville 'our American Crusoe' and finding Fayaway a living manifestation

J. R. Jobbins, 'Escape from the Island', engraving which forms the frontispiece of
The Recreation: A Gift-book for Young Readers (1847). This represents the earliest
published visual image of Herman Melville.

of Byron's lines: 'Would that the desert were my dwelling place, / With one fair spirit for my minister.' The Crusoe comparison is practically ubiquitous in the contemporary reviews. The *New York Herald* called Melville the 'New Robinson Crusoe' and found *Typee* 'written with great elegance and perspicuity'. The *Richmond Enquirer* also compared *Typee* with *Robinson Crusoe*, enjoying 'its free, dashing style, and entertaining narratives and descriptions'.[15]

Though flattered by the comparison to Daniel Defoe's masterpiece, Melville would distance himself from *Robinson Crusoe* with his own masterpiece. In *Moby-Dick* Ishmael explains why he refuses to sail as a passenger: 'For to go as a passenger you must needs have a purse, and a purse is but a rag unless you have something in it.'[16] Ishmael's refusal repudiates Crusoe's statement that he never goes to sea as a sailor: 'Having money in my pocket, and good clothes upon my back, I would always go on board in the habit of a gentleman.'[17] Going beyond *Robinson Crusoe*, *Moby-Dick* celebrates the physical labour of the working man but also emphasizes the hard work the life of the mind entails.

Gansevoort sent Herman all the London reviews he encountered, but his latest set of reviews came with a depressing letter admitting he was so ill that, though only thirty, he had almost lost the will to live. Upon receiving the letter, Herman sent his ailing brother a cheery response.[18] By the time Herman's letter arrived Gansevoort was dead.

The third week of June 1846 Herman left Lansingburgh for New York to meet the ship carrying his brother's remains. While waiting, he came across more *Typee* reviews. The book had run its course in the dailies, but now the monthlies were having their say. The Protestant Church, which controlled a large segment of the American periodical press, had vested interests in the success of the South Pacific missions. The *New-York Evangelist*, a Congregational weekly, condemned *Typee*.[19] John Wiley never really liked the book his partner had accepted for publication. A good Presbyterian,

Wiley agreed with the criticism coming from the religious press. He subjected Melville to a 'fiery ordeal', urging him to prepare a second edition and neutralize his attacks on the missionaries. Melville painfully complied.[20]

Herman had Gansevoort's remains transported to Uncle Peter's home in Albany, where the funeral took place. Maria Melville sorted through his belongings and found her husband's watch fob, which she had given to Gansevoort. Now she gave it to her next oldest son. The family's welfare would depend on Herman now.[21]

Two months after Gansevoort's death, Julia Melvill died of tuberculosis, following her father, who had died of natural causes the previous summer. Julia was on Herman's mind as he wrote his next book. Fictionalizing the story of his adventures aboard the *Lucy Ann* for *Omoo*, he decided against using the ship's real name and sought an apt substitute. He could think of no better name than that of his favourite cousin. He christened the ship *Julia*.

Read in light of Melville's life, every mention of *Julia* or 'Little Jule', as the sailors in *Omoo* call their ship, pays homage to his cousin. The words the narrator uses to describe the ship – 'poor little Jule', 'brave little Jule' – could be words the family used to describe Julia Melvill in her final illness. When he and his shipmates watch the *Julia* sail from Tahiti, the narrator describes its departure in a tone of profound melancholy that resonated in the family: 'Thus disappeared little Jule, about three weeks after entering the harbor; and nothing more have I ever heard of her.'[22]

The narration in *Omoo* is fairly straightforward, but occasionally Melville adopts a contemplative mood similar to what he used in the penultimate chapter of *Typee*. Describing his hero's arrival at Papeetee, for example, he conveys the experience as a layered memory. On the beach his fictional alter ego sees the wrecked hull of an American whaling ship. When he views the wreck, it unleashes a flood of emotion-packed memories:

Before leaving Tahiti, I had the curiosity to go over this poor old ship, thus stranded on a strange shore. What were my emotions, when I saw upon her stern the name of a small town on the river Hudson! She was from the noble stream on whose banks I was born; in whose waters I had a hundred times bathed. In an instant, palm-trees and elms – canoes and skiffs – church spires and bamboos – all mingled in one vision of the present and the past.[23]

One image blends several moments from the narrator's life: his arrival at Papeetee, the day he examined the wreck and the boyhood he spent on the Hudson River, itself a matrix of personal memories. For Melville individual memories coalesced to create complex, layered memories that juxtapose disparate moments from his personal past.

Little evidence survives to document Melville's composition of *Omoo*, but his correspondence reveals he took great pride in what he wrote, took offence when publishers suggested cuts and took measures to restore excised text. Melville had included an erotic dance scene in the *Typee* manuscript he had submitted to John Murray. Henry Milton had cut it. Melville resented the revision but held onto the episode and put it into his next book. Sending Murray *Omoo*, Melville justified the inclusion, arguing that Tahitian dance closely resembles Marquesan dance. Murray left it in *Omoo*.[24] Reading Melville's depiction of native dancing girls, one can see why a publisher might object:

Presently, raising a strange chant, they softly sway them-selves, gradually quickening the movement, until, at length, for a few passionate moments, with throbbing bosoms and glowing cheeks, they abandon themselves to all the spirit of the dance, apparently lost to every thing around.[25]

Miss Whieldon never told him about dances like these.

The charm of *Omoo* goes beyond titillation. It takes the same narrative approach as *Typee*. Flâneur-like, the narrator describes island life while leisurely strolling around the island. He records whatever grabs his attention and ponders its meaning. Melville himself said *Omoo* portrayed 'the "man about town" sort of life, led, at the present day, by roving sailors in the Pacific'.[26] Much of the humour in this very funny book comes from the way its narrator ironically assumes a sophisticated air to comment on what he sees while island hopping through the South Pacific.

Melville considered *Omoo* 'a fitting successor to *Typee*'. Whereas his first book depicts Polynesian life in its primitive state, the second shows it 'as affected by intercourse with the whites'.[27] *Typee* opposes whites and Polynesians. Though Tommo critiques the missionaries, he ultimately must choose between native culture and Western society. Escaping Typee Valley, he returns to Western civilization, which, like it or not, he shares with the missionaries. *Omoo* is culturally more complex. Portraying Polynesian life as influenced by Western culture, Melville depicts natives who have been corrupted by visiting missionaries. He also portrays sailors who have abandoned the commercial ships that symbolize Western culture in favour of an uncertain existence in the netherworld between civilized and primitive.

Throughout the composition of *Omoo* Melville concentrated on the task at hand, refusing to let current events distract him. It was difficult to do, considering that the u.s. went to war against Mexico in 1846. Scattered references in his subsequent writings indicate the Mexican War's impact on him. The conflict started with Texas. Mexico, which had never acknowledged the sovereignty of the Republic of Texas, subsequently refused to acknowledge Texas as a u.s. territory after its annexation in 1845. Mexico also disputed the southern border of Texas, claiming it only extended to the Nueces River, not the Rio Grande.

In January 1846 President Polk ordered General Zachary Taylor to lead his troops through the disputed region to the Rio Grande, which Mexico viewed as an act of hostile aggression. In the fourth week of April Mexican cavalry crossed the Rio Grande above Matamoros and ambushed a scouting party of Taylor's dragoons, killing eleven soldiers and taking dozens of American troops prisoner. Polk asked the House of Representatives and the Senate to declare war.

Mexican forces, though numerically superior, could not halt the American advance. Taylor's army crossed the Rio Grande and conquered much of northern Mexico. In the third week of September 1846 U.S. forces reached the outskirts of Monterrey or 'Monterey', as the American press spelled the capital of Nuevo León. The ensuing battle inspired the greatest poem to emerge from the Mexican War. Charles Fenno Hoffman's 'Monterey' is his masterpiece. Melville loved it. He read 'Monterey' when it appeared after the battle and practically committed the poem to memory. It would strongly influence his own verse. Decades later Melville could still recall favourite lines from 'Monterey'.[28]

Despite Taylor's success in northern Mexico, his slow progress forced Polk to authorize the opening of another front. General Winfield Scott, who led the advance, decided to land his forces at Veracruz using surfboats that looked strangely familiar to some eyes. These surfboats, Robert Tomes observed, were 'built sharp at either end, somewhat like those used by whalers'.[29] The similarity between the naval surfboats and whaling boats anticipates Melville's playful suggestion in *Moby-Dick* that Mexico is a Loose-Fish – a sovereign land – waiting for the U.S. to make it a Fast-Fish. The landing at Veracruz, which Melville characterized as 'Old Scott's young dash at Mexico', took place on Tuesday, 9 March 1847. Guert Gansevoort participated in the landing; Melville commemorated his cousin's bravery in a narrative poem, 'Bridegroom Dick'.[30]

N. Currier, *Landing of the American Forces under Genl. Scott, at Vera Cruz, March 9th, 1847*, lithograph, *c*. 1847.

Bright and sunny with a favourable breeze from the southeast, that Tuesday was an ideal day for invasion. General W. J. Worth, who was, in Melville's words, 'happy in his surname, though indeed his worth was of another sort than that of the purse', would lead the first landing.[31] Troops piled into the surfboats, which formed themselves in a line before proceeding to shore en masse. Lieutenant Gansevoort commanded one surfboat. Many feared they would face stiff opposition: the dunes behind Collado Beach offered Mexican troops natural cover from which they could fire at will on the Americans.

At 5.30 that afternoon the surfboats headed for shore. According to the military historian Jack Bauer, General Worth was the first man ashore, but an eyewitness tells a different story. General Worth and Lieutenant Gansevoort 'sprung simultaneously from their boats the first to touch the land'.[32] In a matter of moments, hundreds of other troops jumped from their surfboats into the water and waded ashore, all wondering when the Mexicans would fire. Instead of defending Callado Beach and inflicting heavy casualties on the landing force, the Mexicans fled. Tomes explains: 'Not a foe showed himself, to dispute the ground; and the American troops formed upon the neighboring sand-hills, with the quiet and order of a parade in their own country.'[33] By midnight over eight thousand American troops had been put ashore without the loss of a single life.

As the Mexican War continued, Melville stayed focused on his writing. By the end of November 1846 he had nearly completed a draft of *Omoo*, which he took with him to Manhattan. Given Wiley's high-handed treatment of *Typee*, Melville felt no particular loyalty towards his firm. He decided to shop his new manuscript around and approached the Harpers. When Melville arrived at their office with his manuscript, Fletcher Harper had just left the building. The youngest Harper brother, Fletcher took primary responsibility for acquisitions. Frederick Saunders was in the office when Melville arrived. Though he usually displayed proper manners – one friend remembered 'his courtly English civilities' – Saunders had good reason to greet Melville cordially.[34] *Typee*'s success had confirmed Saunders's original opinion and let the Harpers know they had goofed by ignoring his recommendation. Saunders long remembered the conversation that occurred when Melville visited the Harpers' office with his *Omoo* manuscript.[35]

'Saunders, I suppose there is no use of offering this to the house?' Melville said with some hesitance.

'Wait a minute,' Saunders replied. 'Mr Harper is in his carriage now at the door about to start to Europe. I'll go and ask him.'

Without bothering to put on his hat, Saunders rushed outside and caught Fletcher Harper just in time.

'What is it?' Harper asked.

'Oh another manuscript from Herman Melville,' Saunders told him. 'He is offering it to us. What do you say?'

'Take it at once,' Harper said as he jumped into his carriage and drove off.

Murray published the London edition of *Omoo* in March 1847; the New York edition appeared the following month. The reviews

Frederick Saunders, 19th-century, photomechanical print.

were quite positive. *Omoo* did not have a Fayaway, but it did have Doctor Long Ghost, a character many found a lovable scamp.[36] Questions about Melville's authenticity resurfaced. Frederick Hardman also wondered about the dedicatee: 'Of the existence of Uncle [Herman] Gansevoort, of Gansevoort, Saratoga County, we are wholly incredulous.' But Hardman loved Doctor Long Ghost, whom he called 'a jewel of a boy, a complete original, hit off with uncommon felicity'.[37]

Not all readers appreciated the long doctor. Some saw him as a dangerous character. The *New Zealander*, for example, found him representative

> of a class common in all those remote parts of the world, where men either seek to recruit the fortunes and the reputation that have been sacrificed at home, or to plunge still deeper into the reckless desperate, licentious courses that first seduced them from the ordinary and honourable path.[38]

The *New Zealander* recognized Long Ghost as a type of individual who illustrates the depths into which men could sink at the ends of the earth. New Zealand readers preferred a different character in *Omoo*, Benbow Byrne, whom Melville portrayed as a Maori harpooneer.[39]

Friends did what they could to promote *Omoo*. When a mean-spirited review appeared in the Whig press, J. B. Auld refuted it in the Democratic press, explaining, 'We happened, like the vast majority of readers here and abroad, to read *Omoo* with feelings of unmixed delight.'[40] Hoffman began his review by recalling the controversy over *Typee*, which he quickly dismissed. He remembered 'when men used to tell longer and *stronger* stories over their Madeira than is now the fashion among modern sherry drinkers'. *Omoo* is so good, Hoffman argued, that it will encourage people to reread *Typee*. Read Melville once to enjoy his story; read him twice to enjoy his style.[41]

Though the American reviews were largely positive, Christian editors scourged *Omoo*. Their criticism worked to Melville's advantage. The best way to get people to read a book, of course, is to tell them not to. Filling out her editorial miscellany for the August issue of *Union Magazine*, Caroline Kirkland recognized how Christian censure ironically promoted Melville's second book:

Omoo. – A writer in one of the late religious papers complains that, at the recent anniversary meeting of the Foreign Missionary Society, no notice was taken of Mr. Melville's censures of the missionaries at the Sandwich Islands! If we had met with such a suggestion in other quarters, we should certainly have suspected it to be neither more nor less than an ingenious puff of the book.[42]

When Herman was in the South Pacific, his sister Helen had befriended Elizabeth Shaw, the daughter of Lemuel Shaw, chief justice of Massachusetts. As their friendship blossomed, Elizabeth often visited the Melville family in Lansingburgh, sometimes staying for weeks at a time. The whole family liked her. She and Tom, the youngest Melville, shared an interest in collecting, and he presented her with curiosities that she could add to her collection, which included such valuable items as the shaving mug of colonial American poet Mather Byles.[43] Elizabeth's visits to Lansingburgh took on a different tenor once Herman returned from the South Seas. To what extent did her passion for collecting fuel her interest in Helen's exotic brother? What greater curiosity could she add to her personal collection than the new Robinson Crusoe, a man who had lived among cannibals, especially one who was handsome, intelligent and, like Helen, had a wry, quick-witted sense of humour?

Becoming engaged to a celebrity presented a challenge. Elizabeth had dreamed of getting married in a church, but she and Herman settled on a more private ceremony in the Shaws' Boston home on Beacon Hill. The family had decided against a church wedding because they feared that if news about the wedding of 'Typee' got out a big crowd would gather outside the church to see him.[44]

Melville's engagement to Elizabeth Shaw brought him into contact with some of the leading lights of Boston society, none more

Caroline Kirkland, 1856, wood engraving.

significant than her father. Shaw had been engaged to Herman's
Aunt Nancy, who died before they could wed. He later married
Elizabeth's mother but never forgot his first love. Shaw assumed a
role as protector for the Melvilles. His daughter's engagement to
Nancy's nephew reinforced his commitment to the family. One of
Boston's most distinguished citizens, Shaw had been serving as
chief justice since 1830. He looked the part. Shaw had a large, square
head that seemed as if it had been chiselled from a block of granite
from which only a few chips had been removed. But he would
always have a soft spot in his heart for a man named Melville.

The eve of the wedding the Shaws and the Melvilles attended a
party with many of Boston's leading citizens. Herman disliked big
social gatherings, but the guests that night included Richard Henry

Dana Jr. The author of *Typee* and the author of *Two Years before the Mast* could talk to one another and let the other guests do as they pleased. Melville's conversation astonished Dana, who found him 'incomparable in dramatic story telling'.[45]

On 4 August, their wedding day, Melville took a contemplative stroll, his last as a bachelor. Walking through a grassy area, presumably the Boston Common, he spied a four-leaf clover.[46] He shared the discovery with his bride, the collector of curiosities. A four-leaf clover found by chance on her wedding day would make a delightful addition to any bride's collection. Every year on their anniversary Herman would remind Elizabeth about his lucky discovery. Some years his reminder took on a tinge of irony.

4

The Fight of All Fights

After their wedding dinner Herman and Elizabeth Melville
boarded the train to New Hampshire to start their honeymoon.
Steamer service across Lake Winnipesaukee would not begin
for two years, so they took a coach from the railroad's northern
terminus to Center Harbor, the lakeside resort town where they
would spend the next few nights. Nearly everyone who came
to Center Harbor stayed at Senter House: 'Here one meets with
all classes of society, from mechanics to millionaires – from
brainless coxcombs to men of letters – from mad-cap girls to
managing mammas.' Senter House supplied all the facilities the
newlyweds needed, whether they wanted to go boating, fishing or
horseback riding.[1]

Leaving Center Harbor, the Melvilles travelled through Saco
Valley, which Herman would recall in *Moby-Dick*. Ishmael imagines
an artist who strives to paint 'the dreamiest, shadiest, quietest,
most enchanting bit of romantic landscape in all the valley of the
Saco'. They spent several days in the White Mountains, the very
name of which, as Melville says in 'The Whiteness of the Whale',
casts a 'gigantic ghostliness over the soul'. Elsewhere he calls the
cloud-covered view from Mount Washington, the tallest peak in the
White Mountains, 'a view of hell from Abraham's bosom'.[2]

Though she enjoyed Montreal, Elizabeth found Quebec City
intimidating. Looking down from the ramparts onto Lower Town
– the commercial district – they realized the immense height of the

fortifications. Quebec reminded Herman of his time in the navy. In *White-Jacket* he would call the man-of-war 'a lofty, walled, and garrisoned town, like Quebec, where the thoroughfares are mostly ramparts, and peaceable citizens meet armed sentries at every corner'.[3] One aspect of the sentries caught Elizabeth's eye: 'Every few steps you encounter a sentry in full Highland costume bare knees and all.' Though a worldly married woman of nearly three weeks, she could hardly stand the sight of the Highlanders' bald pink knees. Herman admired them. In *Mardi* he would explain how the Highlander bared the knee 'in token that it was honorable as the face, since it had never been bent'.[4]

Elizabeth also had a problem with their accommodations in Quebec. She wrote her stepmother:

> The House at which we are staying, the best one in the place, is a great rambling, scrambling old castle of a thing, all stairs and entries, and full of tawdry decorations. A forbidding *strangeness* pervades the place and makes one want to get out of it as soon as possible.[5]

Forget the quality of their hotel: look at the quality of Elizabeth's writing. No wonder she fell for a writer and he for her. With him in Lansingburgh and her in Boston, they had carried out their courtship through the mail. Their courtship correspondence does not survive: a great loss to American literature. Elizabeth's ability to turn a phrase had turned Herman's head.

The wet weather made Canada a grey and gloomy place. One day they took advantage of a break in the rain to visit the Plains of Abraham, where General Wolfe defeated the French at the cost of his life during the Seven Years' War. Before leaving Quebec for Lansingburgh, where they would become part of Maria Melville's household, they bought some souvenirs, including a meerschaum pipe for Herman.[6] Made from a type of white clay known as sea foam, the meerschaum develops a rich patina, acquiring a darker hue and a deeper tone as it is smoked. Over time, the bowl of a meerschaum becomes a history of its use.

In Lansingburgh Melville knew he had to get back to *Mardi*, the work he had started writing earlier that year. He remained unsure how to shape it. He considered following the pattern of his earlier books, resuming the story where *Omoo* left off and taking it to Hawaii. Instead he found himself writing an adventurous tale about jumping ship and escaping in an open boat in the middle of the Pacific.

As *Mardi* begins the narrator and a Skyeman named Jarl encounter Samoa and his wife Annatoo. Samoa loses an arm and then his wife, establishing a pattern of loss that would persist throughout *Mardi*. The narrator rescues a fair maiden named Yillah from sacrifice. They reach Mardi, a fictional Polynesian archipelago, where the narrator poses as a demigod named Taji. When Yillah mysteriously disappears, Taji begins a quest throughout Mardi to find her, accompanied by King Media and his entourage, which includes Mohi, a historian; Babbalanja, a philosopher; and Yoomy, a minstrel. The novel's loose, episodic structure let Melville go this way and that on the slightest whim, which ideally suited his burgeoning literary ambitions.

Reversing the proverbial dictum requiring a man to put something into his pipe for the purpose of smoking it, Melville decided to put his pipe into something: his book. The main characters regale themselves with a kind of pipe they call 'Froth-of-the-Sea'. They discuss what makes the pipe superior to others. The process of smoking imparts flavour and character to the bowl, they decide. King Media puts it simply: 'The older the better.'[7] From Melville's perspective King Media's maxim applies to much beyond meerschaum pipes. To give his writing a patina akin to the colouration of a well-used meerschaum Melville saw as one of the most difficult tasks he faced as an author.

After growing up a pampered child in Boston, Elizabeth had trouble adjusting to life in Lansingburgh. Though she had spent much time at the Melville home over the past few years, Elizabeth had always been a houseguest. Now she was expected to do her domestic duties like her sisters-in-law. Judge Shaw devised a solution to get his daughter, her husband and all the other Melvilles out of Lansingburgh and back to New York. He would give his son-in-law $2,000 to lease a house in the city. Herman's brother Allan and his new bride would join them. Since Allan Melville's law office was prospering, he could help share expenses. Save for Thomas, who was at sea, all the Melvilles would be reunited under one roof.

They found a suitable home at 103 Fourth Avenue, between Eleventh and Twelfth Streets. A fairly new property, it lacked the stateliness of the New York homes where the Melvilles had lived before fleeing to Albany. The new house was roomy enough for the family, even as it expanded during the early years of both marriages. Almost four times deep as wide, the three-storey house had a large parlour on the first floor for entertaining with a second, smaller parlour for more intimate gatherings.[8]

Melville entered the city's leading literary circles. He often visited Dr John W. Francis, a catalyst for New York intellectual life whose home on Bond Street was a gathering place for everyone from poets to professors. Generous with his hospitality and his opinions, Francis impressed the men and charmed the women who visited. Edgar Allan Poe recorded how Francis 'pats every lady on the head and (if she be pretty and *petite*) designates her by some such title as "My Pocket Edition of the Lives of the Saints"'.[9]

His storytelling ability made Melville a welcome guest at Francis's home. Augustus Gardner, who befriended him there, found Melville 'taciturn, but genial, and when warmed-up, capitally racy and pungent'.[10] Though one of the best testimonies of Melville's storytelling ability, Gardner's account suffers the same problem as so many others: he never transcribed any of Melville's stories. Another

Mathew B. Brady, *Dr John Francis*, *c*. 1850, daguerreotype.

friend, N. P. Willis, identified *Typee* and *Omoo* as 'conversational literature', implying that they sounded like their author talked, but Gardner's modifiers suggest that Melville sometimes said in person what he could not say in print. For want of a Boswell nearly all the stories Melville told in conversation have been lost.

Gowans' Bookstore, then located on the upper floor at 63 Liberty Street, became another favourite hangout. This year Melville purchased from Gowans a London edition of Robert Burton's *Melancholy*. The store's dingy aisles adversely affected Melville's choice. Not until he got home did he realize it was a poorly selected and edited version of Burton that did little to preserve the quality of the original. When Wiley and Putnam published a fuller and more reliable edition of Burton, Melville acquired a copy of the new edition and ignored the one he got from Gowans.[11]

That Melville was visiting antiquarian bookstores and reading seventeenth-century classics shows his literary curiosity deepening as his literary ambition soared. Though he had known about Burton's *Anatomy of Melancholy* since 'Fragments from a Writing Desk', he had never read it closely or used it as a model. Now he would. In the opening chapter of *Mardi* Taji pines for someone 'who could page me a question from Burton on Blue Devils'.[12] Though a direct reference to *Anatomy of Melancholy*, this comment shows little knowledge of its contents. As *Mardi* progressed Melville's debt to Burton would become increasingly apparent.

In the 'Time and Temples' chapter, Taji argues that great monuments take time to construct. For proof he offers an astonishing catalogue of so-called temples. Some examples derive from a similar catalogue in *Anatomy of Melancholy*. Not only did Melville borrow specific references from Burton, he adopted his technique of heaping one example atop another to create an extraordinary progression that builds to a crescendo.

The lengthy negative catalogue in 'Time and Temples' presents variations on the proverb 'Rome wasn't built in a day'. It begins:

> Nero's House of Gold was not raised in a day; nor the
> Mexican House of the Sun; nor the Alhambra; nor the
> Escurial; nor Titus's Amphitheater; nor the Illinois
> Mounds; nor Diana's great columns at Ephesus.[13]

The references to Nero's house, the temple of Diana at Ephesus and
the Escurial palace near Madrid all come from Burton.[14] Melville
added originality partly by introducing New World examples,
including the Pyramid of the Sun at Teotihuacan – the religious
centre of the Toltec civilization near Mexico City – and North
American Indian mounds.

Developing the catalogue further, he mixed additional examples
from Old World and New, also contrasting the natural and the
man-made:

> Round and round, the Moorish turret at Seville was not
> wound heavenward in the revolution of a day; and from its
> first founding, five hundred years did circle, ere Strasbourg's
> great spire lifted its five hundred feet into the air. No: nor
> were the great grottos of Elephanta hewn out in an hour;
> nor did the Troglodytes dig Kentucky's Mammoth Cave in a
> sun; nor that of Trophonius, nor Antiparos; nor the Giant's
> Causeway. Nor were the subterranean arched sewers of
> Etruria channeled in a trice, nor the airy arched aqueducts
> of Nerva thrown over their vallies in the ides of a month.
> Nor was Virginia's Natural Bridge worn under in a year.[15]

Melville would apply a similar pattern in *Moby-Dick,* often
following an example from the Old World with one from the
New, placing both on the same level and blurring the boundaries
between them.

Late in 'Time and Temples' Melville puts literature among
the monuments that take time to create, suggesting that the best

Virginia's Natural Bridge was a favourite image for Melville. He would later compare the sight of Moby Dick as it surfaced to this famous geological formation.

books would endure beyond architectural temples: 'Nor were the parts of the great *Iliad* put together in haste; though old Homer's temple shall lift up its dome, when St. Peter's is a legend.'[16] After the catalogue, the reader feels a dizzying rush, but Melville hardly seems out of breath. He pauses to make a richly evocative generalization:

> Thus deeper and deeper into Time's endless tunnel, does the winged soul, like a night-hawk, wend her wild way; and finds eternities before and behind; and her last limit is her everlasting beginning.[17]

The chapter's conclusion is understated. With a closing metaphor comparing Time to Alaric, the King of the Visigoths who sacked Rome in the fifth century, Melville emphasizes that, paradoxically, Time is the destroyer of temples as well as their builder. A briefer and simpler catalogue offers a series of appositives describing Time, all linked together with a repetitive conjunction. The closing passage meditates like a metronome, casting the reader into a mesmeric spell: 'Thus, then, though Time be the mightiest of Alarics, yet is he the mightiest mason of all. And a tutor, and a counselor, and a physician, and a scribe, and a poet, and a sage, and a king.'[18]

Few places in New York lured Melville inside its doors more often than Evert Duyckinck's home at 20 Clinton Place. A congenial host, Duyckinck invited like-minded souls to gather at 'Number Twenty', where Melville met the nation's leading literati. Cornelius Mathews, for one, was always welcome. A great conversationalist, Mathews could talk your leg off. Some wished he could write as well as he talked. South Carolina author William Gilmore Simms stopped by Number Twenty while visiting New York in the mid-1840s and met the author of *Typee* many times.[19] Occasionally Duyckinck visited Melville, whose home he found congenial and intellectually stimulating.

Mathew B. Brady, *Cornelius Mathews*, *c*. 1850, daguerreotype.

Melville and Duyckinck also met elsewhere. On the evening of 6 October 1847 they came together at the gallery of the American Art Union on Broadway for its grand opening. Interested parties could subscribe to the Art Union for five dollars per share. The funds were used to purchase paintings and other works of art from the finest artists in the nation. The Art Union benefited both painter and patron. It gave many art lovers an opportunity to own works they could not have afforded otherwise, broadening the art market beyond the wealthy. Though based in New York, the American Art Union aggressively sought subscribers across the nation. In Toledo, Ohio, for example, Charles M. Dorr – a future mayor – subscribed for a share.[20]

'Distribution of the American Art Union Prizes', *c.* 1848, print.

The grand opening of the new gallery was a gala affair. Admission was by invitation only, and attendees were treated to a supper of cold chicken, oysters and champagne. Duyckinck was happy to show the author of *Typee* around. Melville met Charles Lanman, whose painting *Red Sandstone Bluffs, Lake Superior* was being exhibited in the new gallery. Lanman introduced Duyckinck and Melville to William S. Mount, a Long Island painter best known for his genre paintings, one of which, *The Novice*, was on display.[21]

Melville enjoyed Frederic Edwin Church's painting *The Charter Oak, at Hartford* so much he wrote it into *Mardi*. The oak belonged to local legend. In 1687 Governor Edmund Andros demanded that Hartford colonists surrender the Connecticut charter. They refused, hiding it in the hollow of a white oak tree. In an extraordinary set of personal statements placing himself at key moments throughout history in the 'Faith and Knowledge' chapter,

Taji says, 'I am he, that from the king's minions hid the Charter in the old oak at Hartford.'[22]

To tell the Shaws in Boston how the Melvilles in New York lived Elizabeth wrote a letter to her stepmother describing a typical day in their lives. After having breakfast at eight o'clock, Herman took the first of three daily walks, leaving Elizabeth home to straighten their suite of rooms. Their bedroom doubled as her room and a private sitting room. An adjoining chamber served as his writer's room, where he enclosed himself after his morning walk. With neither stove nor fireplace, the room could get quite cold in the winter. Herman, who loved the change of seasons, did not mind. He bundled himself in blankets to stay warm enough to write his latest tale of the tropics.[23]

Herman liked to walk for an hour or more after lunch. Rain or snow hardly mattered: he went out in all conditions. If the weather was nice, Elizabeth accompanied him. Together they walked a couple of miles down Broadway, staying out until two, when Herman went upstairs to resume his work. They dined at four. After dinner the couple went to their bedroom for a chat. Sometimes he read to her from what he had written that day. After their time together, Herman went for another walk, often visiting a reading room to peruse the evening papers. He sometimes attended book auctions as a pleasant diversion. It was during these evening walks that he stopped by Bond Street or Clinton Place.

Melville usually returned home before eight. His weak eyes prevented him from reading or writing by candlelight. Sometimes he and Elizabeth played whist with two other willing family members. Most evenings the family gathered in the parlour. One person would read, the rest listen. Charles Dickens was everyone's favourite author for parlour reading. Like other authors whose works Melville encountered during the composition of *Mardi*, Dickens influenced his writing style. The long conversations between Mohi, Yoomy and Babbalanja, as Leonard Woolf noticed, resemble those of Dickens when he 'is really letting himself go'.[24] The family would disperse around ten o'clock, seldom later. If Herman did not get a good night's sleep, he could not concentrate on his writing the next day.

The compositional method Melville had developed with *Typee* and *Omoo* would not work for *Mardi*. He did not need recent voyages for models; he needed timeless classics. One batch of books Duyckinck loaned him reveals the direction Melville was taking. Rabelais' rollicking satirical opus *Gargantua and Pantagruel* provided a structural and stylistic model. But Sir Thomas Browne offered Melville what he wanted most: a way to make prose sound like poetry.

Browne uses purposeful redundancy, playing with words to create paradoxical aphorisms, often structured chiastically. So does Melville. At one point, Babbalanja speaks of 'a mystery within the obvious, yet an obviousness within the mystery'. Browne incorporates numerous conjoined word pairs, sometimes putting several into a single sentence. So does Melville. To explain how Samoa ('the Upoluan') became more insightful once they land, Taji says: 'But our craft *high and dry*, the Upoluan lifted his crest as the erudite pagan; master of *Gog and Magog*, expounder of all things *heathenish and obscure.*'[25]

With the capacity to sustain a rhythm over the course of a paragraph or a series of paragraphs, Browne gave his prose poetic qualities. Melville's elegant balance and use of parallel construction in 'Time and Temples' recall Browne's style:

> And that which long endures full-fledged, must have long
> lain in the germ. And duration is not of the future, but
> of the past; and eternity is eternal, because it has been;
> and though a strong new monument be builded today,
> it only is lasting because its blocks are old as the sun.[26]

N. Currier, *Steam Ship Washington: Belonging to the Ocean Steam Navigation Company, Frederick Hewitt Commander*, 1847, lithograph. This presents an image of the sister ship of the *Hermann*, the ship Melville toured with his friend, the ship's surgeon, Robert Tomes.

Whereas Melville's sources for *Typee* and *Omoo* had given him facts and incidents, his sources for *Mardi* gave him a sense of style.

Sometimes Melville and Duyckinck explored the city together. They shared an interest in transatlantic travel. Earlier Duyckinck had spent two days aboard the *Washington*, a new liner of the Ocean Steamer Navigation Company, during its trial run. In the third week of March 1848 they visited the *Hermann*, its sister ship. Theirs was no chance visit: they had been invited aboard by Robert Tomes, who had taken a position as permanent surgeon aboard the *Hermann*.[27] The first ocean liners constructed with double engines, the *Washington* and *Hermann* excelled all other steamships plying the passenger trade across the Atlantic. Stepping aboard the *Hermann*, people quickly saw how luxurious it was. Why, it had a dance hall that was large enough for mazurkas, polkas, quadrilles and waltzes. Melville sometimes questioned the necessity of steam-powered travel, but the *Hermann* was an awe-inspiring symbol of what modern man could create.[28]

A letter Melville wrote Murray forms the fullest documentary evidence that *Mardi* had undergone a major change of focus by the end of March 1848. It also illustrates Melville's wanton neglect of the circumstances of publication. Ignoring Murray's aversion to novels, Melville made a case for *Mardi*. Since so many readers had assumed *Typee* and *Omoo* were fictional, Melville wanted to write a novel to show what he could really do with the written word. Non-fiction, he argued, had tied his hands, but fiction gave him the freedom to develop his literary potential.

Wrongly assuming that Murray's prejudice against fiction stemmed from a dislike of current sentimental novels, Melville distinguished *Mardi* from other contemporary works of fiction: 'My romance I assure you is no dish water nor its model borrowed from the Circulating Library.' He then offered a brief description of its contents, explaining that it opens like a true narrative but as its romance and poetry grow it becomes a wild tale rich with meaning. Melville applied his debating skills, pre-empting objections as he argued his case. Foreseeing that Murray would object to an author of supposedly true travels switching genres in mid-career, Melville emphasized that *Mardi* would excel his earlier works 'as a literary achievement'. His words mark one of Melville's earliest statements regarding his writerly ambitions. No longer considering his books as things of the moment, he was starting to see his writings as works of art built to last.[29] Murray's reply does not survive, but Melville's subsequent response indicates its icy tone. Murray showed little interest in *Mardi*, but Melville was determined to send him the proofsheets, hoping he would relax his bias against fiction.[30]

'The book is done now': so wrote Elizabeth to her stepmother in early May 1848. Her letter reveals Herman's method as a work approached completion. Saying the book was done, she meant he had completed a near-final draft and given it to her and his sisters to recopy into a legible manuscript suitable for submission to a publisher. Copying Herman's words, they corrected his spelling but omitted all punctuation, letting him supply it as he reread the manuscript. Since Melville, in Leonard Woolf's words, 'bespatters his sentences with semi-colons without regard to meaning or convention', he may not have been the best one to punctuate his prose.[31]

In a follow-up letter Elizabeth revealed another aspect of Herman's compositional process. Discussing the possibility of coming to Boston that summer, she expressed her reluctance to leave New York without her husband. She exclaimed, 'I'm afraid to trust him to finish up the book without me!'[32] Elizabeth was right to worry. Leaving him alone to read the manuscript, she feared he would tinker too much with his text. When Elizabeth went to Boston that summer, Herman, sure enough, expanded his text significantly, developing a detailed allegory by adding episodes inspired by current affairs that satirized political leaders around the globe.

Herman left New York in mid-July to join Elizabeth in Boston. Hosting a party one night, her father invited Dana so he and Herman could get reacquainted. Dana, in turn, hosted a get-together at Parker House in Court Square, treating Melville and a handful of other literary friends to 'cold birds, fruit champagne, and hock'.[33] Eager to continue his manuscript, Melville did not stay in Boston too long. He returned to New York in time for the wedding between Thomas Low Nichols and Mary Gove, who were married on 29 July 1848 in a Swedenborgian ceremony.

Melville continued expanding *Mardi* into the autumn, inserting additional episodes with every breaking news story. When news of the discovery of gold in California reached New York in September, for example, he drafted a gold rush episode for *Mardi*. Altogether, Melville added approximately 25 chapters to a book his wife considered finished. He hardly knew when to stop. Since the subject of *Mardi* is, in Borges's felicitous phrase, 'an infinite chase on an infinite sea', the work did not lend itself to easy conclusion.[34] Melville's inability to let go is essentially an inability to stem the unceasing flow of ideas, memories and texts that came to mind.

Besides all the current events chapters, Melville also added a lengthy dialogue discussing the compositional process of Lombardo, a poet whose *Koztanza* is *Mardi's* great national epic. The dialogue suggests that no one really knew what went on inside his writer's room at 103 Fourth Avenue. Once Elizabeth closed the door and Herman started writing, he poured himself, heart and soul, into the book. The psychic energy he expelled as he wrote would take a heavy toll.

The creative process demands extraordinary intensity, and every serious writer must meet the demand and keep writing regardless of personal cost: 'We must feel our hearts hot – hissing in us. And ere their fire is revealed, it must burn its way out of us; though it consume us and itself.'[35] For Melville, the writing process was tantamount to war, a war with the self, but it was a just war, one worth the arduous struggle, one that would yield a result destined to last the ages. Channelling Lombardo, Babbalanja states, 'The fight of all fights is to write.'[36]

Babbalanja's statement reinforces the parallel between the writer's struggle and Taji's quest. As he expanded the book in the summer of 1848, Melville bought a copy of Dante's *Divine Comedy*, which helped him imbue *Mardi* with the mythic significance he sought.[37] In the final chapter Taji's companions urge him to stay with them on Serenia, but he resolves to continue his quest. Responding to Mohi's plea, Taji asks: 'Is a life of dying worth living o'er again? – Let *me*, then, be the unreturning wanderer. The helm! By Oro, I will steer my own fate, old man. – Mardi, farewell!'[38]

Albert Camus, who called Melville 'the Homer of the Pacific', compared Taji to Ulysses but acknowledged that the comparison was imprecise because Taji never goes home.[39] As an 'unreturning wanderer', Taji more closely resembles Dante's Ulysses. In Canto XXVI of the *Inferno*, Dante and his guide Virgil descend to the eighth circle of Hell, where they encounter Ulysses. Instead of relating the story of his slow return to Ithaca, Dante's Ulysses describes a final voyage away from home into untravelled seas. Ulysses' story from the *Inferno* has no precedent in classical mythology, but in the nineteenth century it helped Tennyson begin 'Ulysses' and Melville finish *Mardi*.

The second week of November the Harpers offered Melville a contract for *Mardi*. He accepted their offer and the $500 advance that went with it. By the end of January *Mardi* was in proofs. Having forewarned Murray, Melville sent him the proofsheets. Murray did not reject the manuscript without consideration. He handed it to Henry Milton, who spent nine hours reading the proofs, time enough to make the acquaintance of the exotic island princess Yillah and realize *Mardi* was not for Murray.[40]

Melville's London representative next brought *Mardi* to Richard Bentley, who handed the page proofs to his reader, a miscellaneous author named Martha Jones. Since Bentley asked her to expedite the report on *Mardi*, she read two-thirds of it and then skipped to the conclusion. While finding Melville's language 'a little Carlylish', she enjoyed his vivid description. The more Martha Jones read, however, the less she liked *Mardi*, finding that its 'brilliancy of colouring' wearied the senses: 'Here is too little dinner, and too much dessert.' In its second half she found Melville's writing absolutely wild. The 'Dreams' chapter, for example, seemed 'written by a madman'.[41]

Though Bentley generally took Jones's advice, he accepted *Mardi* for publication despite her misgivings. Bentley wanted to add Melville to his list of authors so much he was willing to accept *Mardi*, not necessarily on its own merits but on the strength of the reputation Melville had established with his two previous books. By publishing *Mardi*, Bentley would help secure his subsequent works. He agreed to Melville's terms: two hundred guineas in advance.

When the London edition appeared on 15 March 1849, *Mardi* met with mixed reviews. *The Standard* greeted it warmly. Though

A. Oakey Hall, 1874, wood engraving.

its reviewer could not quite follow the whole story, the occasional obscurities did not prevent an intensely enjoyable reading experience:

> *Mardi* is certainly, for imagination, for picturesque beauties, for profound thought and eloquence, mixed up occasionally with soarings in which we confess we cannot follow him, one of the most interesting and remarkable books to which our attention has been called for a long time. There are pictures for the poet and painter, profound thought for the philosopher, curious speculations for the students of human character, and entertainment for those who seek to be amused.[42]

Other British reviewers enjoyed the literary power of certain chapters like 'Faith and Knowledge' and 'Time and Temples' but found the allegory confusing and the plot poorly developed. Some parodied *Mardi*. *Man in the Moon*, a humorous London magazine edited by Angus Bethune Reach, spoofed Melville's ornate language and elaborate literary references.[43]

Elsewhere in the empire readers enjoyed *Mardi*. A Montreal reviewer observed:

> Herman Melville, in spite of his romantic name, will be not
> an unworthy rival of the most celebrated American novel-
> ists, and his *Mardi* will lift him at once up many steps of
> the ladder, which he has stoutly determined to climb.

Melville's 'racy vigour' this Canadian reader found 'both pleasant and piquant'. Though Murray had considered *Mardi* unsuitable for his Home and Colonial Library, *Mardi* appealed to colonial readers, who found Melville's typename for Great Britain – Dominora – absolutely appropriate.[44]

American reviewers savaged *Mardi*. After many negative reviews, A. Oakey Hall, correspondent of the *New Orleans Commercial Bulletin* and future mayor of New York, sought to staunch the flow. Hall shaped his opinion to suit New Orleans readers, calling *Mardi*

> a regular Mardi-gras of a novel, to judge from the richness
> of its prose. Prose! it is a poem; and you can pencil out of
> its pages blank verse enough to set up an hundred news-
> paper poets, for the balls of bowling critics to roll at.[45]

Hall had no trouble dismissing the contemporary critics, but Melville could not be so flip. Having made up his mind to write books with the power to endure, he was heartbroken by those critics who failed to recognize *Mardi* as a significant advance over his two earlier books. Its adverse reception would, at least temporarily, quash Melville's vaulting ambition and alter the literary course he had set for himself.

5

London

At five o'clock in the morning on 5 November 1849, Captain
Richard Griswold, the skipper of the *Southampton*, a packet ship
on the New York-to-London route, woke his celebrity passenger
to inform him they were off the coast of Dover. Wanting to
travel overland from Dover to London, Melville dressed quickly
and came on deck. A cutter pulled alongside and Melville, with
Prof. George J. Adler and Dr Franklin Taylor, two passengers
he had befriended, scrambled aboard. The boatmen said they
could not land at Dover, only Deal, where the cutter beached at
sunrise. Relating the episode in his journal, Melville wrote: 'Some
centuries ago a person called Julius Caesar jumped ashore about
in this place, and took possession.'[1]

Having left their luggage on the *Southampton*, the three
friends could travel free and easy. Melville proposed they walk
to Canterbury to work up an appetite. The exercise and fresh air
felt great, as did the English ale they drank with breakfast, but
they decided against walking all the way to Canterbury and took
the train. They toured Canterbury Cathedral, where Archbishop
Thomas Becket was slain. Already this trip was paying dividends
in the form of usable imagery. What Melville saw in Canterbury
he would apply in *Moby-Dick* to make the *Pequod* seem as though
it had been roaming the seas for ages on a mythic quest. Ishmael
finds the vessel's ancient decks 'worn and wrinkled, like the pilgrim-
worshipped flag-stone in Canterbury Cathedral where Beckett bled'.[2]

View from Pier E, Deal, England, *c.* 1890, photomechanical print.

Budget travellers all, the three shared a room in Canterbury that night. The next morning they bought third-class tickets on the London train. Melville found lodgings on Craven Street, the same street where Benjamin Franklin had lived in London, which he knew from Franklin's *Autobiography*.[3] Less than two full days in England and already Melville had trod in the same steps as Caesar, Becket and Franklin, personally recapitulating two thousand years of history. From the comfort of Craven Street, but with a twinge of melancholy, he could reflect on what had brought him so far.

Nine months earlier, Melville had been so happy. He and Elizabeth were then in Boston awaiting the birth of their first child and the publication of *Mardi*, the first book that showed what he could really do with the written word. Elizabeth's lying-in period was Herman's lounging-around period. He spent his days in the sumptuous library of her father's Beacon Hill home reading Shakespeare. Having discovered a large-print edition, he delved deeply into Shakespeare's works for the first time. Elizabeth gave birth to a healthy boy. They named him Malcolm – a reflection of his father's recent attention to *Macbeth*. When they left Boston to return to New York the three were very happy. But then the *Mardi* reviews came out. In one fell swoop they dashed Herman's literary ambitions and endangered his hopes of supporting his family as a writer.

The most hurtful review appeared on Thursday, 10 May, the day of the Astor Place Riot. The newspaper containing the review came out in the morning; the riots broke out in the evening. The turmoil in Melville's soul anticipated the turmoil in the city. George Ripley's review appeared on the front page of the *New-York Daily Tribune*. Ripley ripped into *Mardi*, pronouncing the book a failure:

> The story has no movement, no proportions, no ultimate
> end; and unless it is a huge allegory – bits of which peep
> out here and there – winding its unwieldy length along,
> like some monster of the deep, no significance or point.
> We become weary with the shapeless rhapsody, and wonder
> at the audacity of the writer which could attempt such
> an experiment with the long-suffering of his readers.[4]

Melville had genuinely expected *Mardi* to be a critical and commercial success. He thought the reading public would welcome his bravado, his virtuosity and his literary derring-do and rush to bookstores in droves. Ripley recognized the experimental quality of *Mardi*: he just did not like it. In no uncertain terms Ripley let Melville know that he had sorely misjudged his public.

Melville also misjudged the public when it came to the riot. Earlier that week Charles Macready, Britain's leading Shakespearean actor, starred in a performance of *Macbeth* at the Astor Place Opera House. The same night Edwin Forrest, the leading American Shakespearean, performed the same role at the Broadway Theatre. Their rivalry symbolized the conflict between the u.s. and Great Britain, which had never been fully resolved since the War of 1812. It also represented a class struggle, with the working class supporting the American actor and the Anglophilic upper class supporting the British actor. Forrest supporters bought tickets to Macready's performance that night. They smuggled rotten eggs and rotting vegetables into the opera house and pelted the stage with these smelly projectiles while hollering loud enough to drown out the performance.[5]

After that evening's disaster, Macready announced his intention to return to Britain on the next boat. A group of prominent citizens and men of letters signed a petition persuading him to stay and perform. The signatures included Melville's. He was not the only one who misjudged the public's reaction to another performance by Macready. Evert Duyckinck, Washington Irving, Cornelius Mathews and Richard Grant White also signed. James Fenimore Cooper's name is conspicuous by its absence. Cooper understood that his fellow writers were sticking out their necks as they put down their names.[6]

Macready agreed to another performance on the strength of the petition. Oakey Hall, who went to Astor Place that evening, was shocked that the police had not cordoned off the area. Thousands of people stood near the opera house in anticipation. Hall remembered:

> The worst elements of the city were around. Immigrant runners from the First ward, dock thieves from the Third and Fifth wards, rag pickers, bone boilers, sneak thieves, Harlem footpads, Staten Island boatmen, with rowdy fire laddies and roughs burning for fight and plunder, and ready to accept any pretext for disorder, everywhere abounded.[7]

As the riot escalated, the police could not control it, and the state militia took over. Astor Place was close enough to their home that the Melvilles could hear the ruckus – and the gunshots. The militia fired wildly into the uncontrollable crowd, killing a few rioters and several bystanders. Macready escaped the clutches

The Astor Place Riot, 1874, wood engraving.

of the malcontents under the cloak of darkness, fleeing to Boston and, from there, back to England.

In the riot's aftermath Melville settled on a topic for his new book. *Redburn* would treat the subject of U.S. and British relations with sympathy by depicting a young American on his first visit to England. Melville's signature on the Macready petition and the text of *Redburn* both manifest his belief that the language and literary culture the two nations shared should be a bridge towards understanding, something his finest readers have recognized. St Loe Strachey, for one, observed that Melville looked beyond the contemporary animosity between Great Britain and the U.S., feeling that 'on the sea at least, it is the English kin against the world.'[8]

Hunkering down in his writer's room to draft *Redburn*, Melville resented that *Mardi*'s commercial failure had forced him to write a more conventional book. *Redburn* was definitely not what he wanted to write next. Having given his imagination free rein in *Mardi*, he hoped to continue its trajectory. Melville was disappointed that the literary marketplace forced him to revert to a book that was closer to *Typee* or *Omoo*, a fictionalized version of personal experience. Never did Melville recognize how good *Redburn* really is. With little time for background reading he avoided overrelying on source material, as he had in *Typee*. With few written sources handy, he drew upon ideas that had lain fallow in his mind since boyhood. By forcing himself to write quickly and rein in his ambitions, he achieved a level of narrative control with *Redburn* that *Mardi* lacks.

A central problem with *Mardi* is its narrative stance. At the start Taji is a strong first-person narrator: bright, funny, introspective, multifaceted: in many ways he anticipates Ishmael in *Moby-Dick*. Once Taji reaches the Mardian archipelago and begins travelling with King Media, Mohi, Yoomy and Babbalanja, facets of his personality get distributed to the different characters, depriving Taji of his individuality.[9] He devolves into little more than an amanuensis for the others, transcribing what they say but seldom contributing to the conversation. On rare occasions, in such chapters as 'Dreams', 'Faith and Knowledge' and 'Time and Temples', Taji soars to great heights, but in these instances, he still lacks individual character, serving as a mouthpiece for Melville's literary aspirations.

The narrative point of view in *Redburn* let Melville develop the character of his first-person narrator, showing what Wellingborough Redburn was like as a green hand on his first voyage and what he is like years later as he reflects upon his youth. This new approach was a major breakthrough in Melville's art, regardless of whether he realized it at the moment. He would reuse this dual perspective in *White-Jacket* and *Moby-Dick*, further experimenting with its possibilities.

By 5 June 1849 work on *Redburn* had progressed far enough for Melville to approach Richard Bentley with the project. Since Bentley had lost money with *Mardi*, Melville reassured him that *Redburn* would be more successful. He differentiated the two works, explaining that, unlike *Mardi*, *Redburn* was a straightforward narrative: 'no metaphysics, no conic sections, nothing but cakes and ale'. With this reassurance, he requested £150 for the British copyright.[10]

The same day that Melville wrote to Bentley the British Court of Exchequer handed down a decision rendering his request meaningless. The court ruled that a foreign author residing abroad who published a work in Great Britain would not acquire a British copyright.[11] Lord Chief Baron of the Exchequer Frederick Pollock could not fathom how something that resulted from an author's mental labour could be copyrighted. The opinion he wrote denies the concept of intellectual property altogether.

Receiving Melville's letter after Pollock's decision, Bentley faced some tough choices as a publisher. He informed Melville how poorly *Mardi* had been doing and then told him about the court case, a 'drivelling absurdity'. Though Bentley hoped the decision would be overturned, until then it exposed him and other conscientious publishers 'to the risk of attack from any unprincipled persons who may choose to turn Pirate'.[12]

Bentley could not purchase the British copyright at any price. In light of the ruling, there was no such thing for foreign authors in Britain. Committed to publishing the best American writers, Bentley offered Melville an advance of £100. Much less than what Melville wanted, Bentley's risky offer was quite generous in light of the court's decision, which would let any British publisher issue *Redburn* without paying its author tuppence. Melville begrudgingly accepted. Since the Harpers' edition of *Redburn* would be in press the third week of July, Melville informed Bentley that he would send him a set of proofsheets in mid-August.

Almost as soon as he finished *Redburn* Melville began a new book. Oakey Hall reported something extraordinary about Melville's composition of *White-Jacket:* he 'dashed [it] off in a score of sittings'.[13] A score of sittings? Is that even possible? The modern edition of *White-Jacket* runs to four hundred pages, meaning that Melville averaged twenty pages a day throughout its composition. Hall's statistic reflects Melville's profound powers of concentration. When necessary, he could write as long as it was light.

The fact that Melville could write quickly does not mean he would write quickly. Given his druthers, he much preferred a slow, easy-going pace. He understood that great literature required leisure, time enough for authors to turn ideas into words.[14] A comment his eponymous narrator makes late in *White-Jacket* reads like a protest against the pressure under which circumstances forced Melville to write. Describing a place aboard ship where he goes for tranquillity, White Jacket says, 'After hearing my fill of the wild yarns of our top, here would I recline – if not disturbed – serenely concocting information into wisdom.'[15] Calm, leisure, relaxation, serenity: call it what you will, repose was essential to turn the raw material of experience into the stuff of literature.

Regardless of the speed with which he wrote the work, Melville reached a level of quality beyond anything he had so far achieved. *White-Jacket* gave V. S. Pritchett the impression of 'a sensitive man who is in complete possession of himself.'[16] In terms of imagery, figurative language, pace and characterization, *White-Jacket* looks forward to what Melville would accomplish with *Moby-Dick*.

Considering the decision from the Court of Exchequer, Melville knew it would be unnecessarily time-consuming to find a British publisher through the transatlantic mail. He decided to visit London himself to find a new publisher. He also hoped to research *Israel Potter*, which would be partly set in London. In addition he entertained the possibility of extending his trip through Europe to the Holy Land and thus giving himself plenty of new material for future books. That plan depended upon receiving a generous advance from a British publisher.

Well, there was no point sitting around his Craven Street room thinking about what had been or might be. Melville had a whole new city to explore. His first night in London he went to Drury Lane Theatre for a concert. Before the curtain rose, the theatre welcomed patrons to enjoy its reading room, where Melville browsed the latest issues of *Blackwood's* and *Bentley's* to read their reviews of *Redburn*. The effusive notice in *Blackwood's*, which ran to fourteen pages, Melville found laughable.[17]

To its author's amazement *Redburn* reviews would continue to be quite good. The London *Morning Chronicle* thought the book ably accomplished literature's traditional twofold purpose: to delight and instruct. *Redburn* 'abounds in glowing sketches of ocean scenery, and skilful, discriminating, and vigorous delineations of nautical character'. It also shed light on the merchant service, giving British readers a glimpse into a vital industry they took for granted. *Redburn* lacks the glamour and exoticism of *Typee*, but it shows what a good writer could do with a humbler journey.[18]

Redburn also received attention from France. Reviewing *Redburn* for *Revue des deux mondes*, Joseph Milsand found that Melville's sentences rapidly succeed one another on the page, as thoughts succeed one another in the mind. 'Each word is marked with the imprint of a new and lively sensation,' Milsand observed. 'He speculates, he philosophizes, he sings about the destiny of America and the eternal mobility of things.' Overall *Redburn* 'is driven by the storyteller's verve and the author's prestigious, all-powerful vitality'.[19]

After the concert at Drury Lane, which climaxed with a performance of Mendelssohn's 'Scottish' Symphony, Melville stopped by the American Bowling Saloon, which had just opened on the Strand a few months earlier. The owners promoted bowling as an 'exercise unequalled for the preservation of health, and the proper development of the muscular powers'. In terms of the 'beauty of the decorations, the completeness of the accommodation, and the novelty of the workmanship', the American Bowling Saloon was 'unequalled by any Establishment in Europe'.[20]

Given his growing interest in the relationship between the u.s. and Great Britain, Melville was curious to witness this British interpretation of an American pastime. His visit to the American Bowling Saloon also seems personally motivated. Melville loved bowling. White Jacket figuratively uses the contemporary term for a strike – 'a ten-stroke' – to mean any impressive accomplishment.[21] Entering a London bowling alley let Melville recall an earlier time. In *Typee* and *Omoo* he had articulated in embryonic form his concept of layered memories, that is, memories of two or more moments in his life whose similarities caused them to coalesce as a single, complex memory. Visiting the American Bowling Saloon on the Strand, Melville deliberately sought a new experience that would bring an old one to mind, letting him contrast his younger self, a whippersnapper who set pins at a Honolulu bowling alley, with his current self, an established author with an international reputation who was in London seeking a publisher for his fifth book.

Since Bentley could not meet until Monday, 12 November, Melville spent his time until then sightseeing. While crossing over the Thames, he wondered how to put the river into his writing: 'A fine thing might be written about a Blue Monday in November London – a city of Dis (Dante's) clouds of smoke – the damned.'[22] He had in mind Canto viii of the *Inferno,* in which Virgil and Dante cross a filthy lake exuding a noxious odour to reach lower Hell, depicted as a fortified city named for Dis: another name for Pluto, the god of the underworld.

Melville would take his own suggestion. The title character of *Israel Potter* enters London on a Blue November Monday in a chapter titled 'In the City of Dis'. The Thames is a river of death, its arched bridges festoons of black crape. Though *Israel Potter* falls into the genre of historical romance, Melville stripped away all romantic pretence to describe the river in terms that anticipate Émile Zola:

The Thames . . . curdled on between rotten wharves, one
murky sheet of sewerage. Fretted by the ill-built piers,
awhile it crested and hissed, then shot balefully through
the Erebus arches, desperate as the lost souls of the harlots,
who, every night, took the same plunge. Meantime, here
and there, like awaiting hearses, the coal-scows drifted
along, poled broadside, pellmell to the current.[23]

Descending to the underworld himself the following day, Melville
walked from one side of the river to the other via the Thames
Tunnel, an underground passage that had opened six years earlier.
Its interior structure reminded him of a vast ribcage. Walking
through the gaslit tunnel, he imagined passing through the inside
of a whale, either that or a giant. He would use both images in
Moby-Dick. Ishmael compares the whale's length to the tunnel's,
and Captain Ahab imagines an ideal man standing 50 ft (15 m) tall
with a 'chest modelled after the Thames Tunnel'.[24]

Crossing Trafalgar Square countless times, Melville had a good
look at Nelson's Column, just completed earlier that year. The
fog that occasionally obscured the monument only made it more
impressive, providing a facsimile of battle smoke and cannon fire.
In *Moby-Dick* Nelson's Column reminds Ishmael of a whaleman
standing atop a mast-head:

Admiral Nelson, also, on a capstan of gun-metal, stands his
mast-head in Trafalgar Square; and even when most obscured
by that London smoke, token is yet given that a hidden
hero is there; for where there is smoke, must be fire.[25]

The Monday meeting with Bentley went well. When Melville
showed him *White-Jacket*, Bentley liked what he saw. He accepted
the book regardless of the copyright dilemma, offering £200 for a
first printing of a thousand copies. He said they could negotiate for

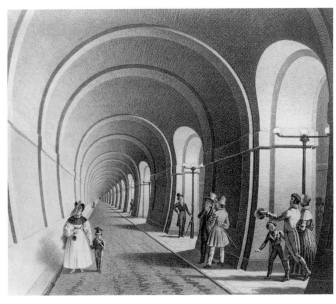

The Thames Tunnel, c. 1850, lithograph.

further remuneration should additional printings prove necessary. The offer was quite liberal, but Bentley hesitated to give him an advance, which is what Melville really wanted. Before accepting Bentley's offer, he decided to approach some other publishers.

While schlepping the proofsheets of *White-Jacket* from one publishing house to another, Melville tried to enjoy London. He discovered some great second-hand bookshops. Walking past the window of Edward Stibbs's shop one day, he noticed a sixteenth-century folio edition of the dramatic works of Francis Beaumont and John Fletcher. When he stepped inside for a closer look, Melville saw that the folio in the window was not the only treasure for sale. Stibbs had thousands of books in stock, including several finely bound and handsomely printed rarities of English literature stretching back to Shakespeare's day. Many British and American collectors knew Stibbs well. Speaking with him, Melville learned that George Duyckinck was a regular customer when he visited London. So was George Putnam. Having split with Wiley, Putnam now had his own publishing house and retail store. He advertised Stibbs's business in the u.s. and imported books from him for New York collectors. Melville bought the Beaumont and Fletcher folio that day, and a Ben Jonson, too.[26]

A few doors down from Stibbs's shop was the Edinburgh Castle, one of several London taverns Melville visited. Its Scottish ale was the best he had ever tasted. The Edinburgh Castle quickly became a finalist in his quest for the perfect snuggery. The dimly lit decor attuned Melville to the imaginative possibilities of such dark and dusky spaces. This and other London taverns Melville visited would influence *Moby-Dick*'s Spouter Inn.

Inside the door of the Edinburgh Castle local tipplers stood at the bar. A narrow passage strewn with sand crunched as patrons squeezed past the bar towards a dining room lined with old-fashioned booths. The booths were a little cramped, which only enhanced their charm. The menu of the Edinburgh Castle – steaks, chops, kidneys, sausages – was renowned, and Londoners considered its pancakes the city's best. The dining room walls were devoid of mirrors and paintings: an aspect of the understated decor Melville appreciated.[27]

Melville kept in touch with George Adler in London. One night they dined together at the Edinburgh Castle. Melville enjoyed 'a glorious chop and a pancake [and] a pint and a half of ale'. A professor at New York University, Adler had recently completed his magnum opus, the 1,400-page *Dictionary of the German and English Language*. This 'formidable lexicon', as Melville called it, would remain the standard work in its field for decades, but, Adler admitted, working on it drove him 'almost crazy'. Beset by paranoid delusions, Adler knew he had endangered his mental health as he compiled the dictionary, but he willingly made the sacrifice, understanding that the creation of a great reference work was a noble endeavour.[28]

Sad to say, Adler's story is not unique. It resembles the plight of Charles Fenno Hoffman, who endangered his mental health 'by too close confinement and incessant application to literary labors'. A literary man with a wounded mind, Hoffman suffered delusions of persecution, becoming convinced someone was trying to poison him. In a lucid moment Hoffman saw himself slipping into a state of delusion and checked into the Pennsylvania Hospital for the Insane.[29]

Melville had learned of Hoffman's situation earlier that year. Writing to Evert Duyckinck, he reflected:

> This going mad of a friend or acquaintance comes straight home to every man who feels his soul in him, – which but few men do. For in all of us lodges the same fuel to light the same fire. And he who has never felt, momentarily, what madness is has but a mouthful of brains. What sort of sensation permanent madness is may be very well imagined . . . It is the climax of a mad night of revelry when the blood has been transmuted into brandy. – But if we prate much of this thing we shall be illustrating our own proposition.[30]

The third week of November Melville visited Greenwich Hospital, the home for pensioners of the Royal Navy. The sight of 1,500 pensioners eating together in the dining hall was something to see. Astonished to find a black man among them, Melville learned that he was from Maryland and had served with Nelson at Trafalgar. Decades later he would include this Baltimore pensioner in *Billy Budd*. Melville's visit to Greenwich Hospital marks a new step in his construction of memory. Whereas his visit to the American Bowling Saloon gave him a way to layer memories from different personal experiences, his conversation with the pensioners let him splice the reminiscences of others onto his own memory, forming connections that personally linked him to history and let Melville extend himself back to a time before he was born.[31]

Seeing a black man among the Greenwich pensioners, Melville made a point to speak with him, learning that he was from Baltimore, Maryland, and that he had fought for Nelson at Trafalgar. When Peter Gansevoort Jr was planning a trip to London, Melville recommended that he see the pensioners and speak with the man from Baltimore. Melville later incorporated the man into *Billy Budd*. *Greenwich Pensioners*, a wood engraving illustrating Max Schlesinger's *Saunterings in and about London*, trans. Otto Wenckstern (1853), facing p. 150, reveals the man also caught the attention of another contemporary traveller.

Henry Stevens, an antiquarian bookdealer from Vermont then working for the British Museum, invited Melville on a private tour of its library. Stevens showed him many rarities up close: the Alexandrine Codex, one of the three oldest Greek manuscripts of the Bible; a unique collection of Anglo-Saxon manuscripts that included *Beowulf*; Charlemagne's Bible; and a copy of John Florio's translation of Montaigne's *Essays* containing the autograph of William Shakespeare, then considered authentic. The experience fired the passion for old books Melville was cultivating in London and reinforced his determination to expand his personal library.

On Tuesday, 27 November, the day after visiting the British Museum Library, Melville left London for Paris. Unable to get an advance on *White-Jacket*, he could not take the journey across Europe to the Holy Land he had projected, but Melville was determined to catch a glimpse of the Continent. From Paris he travelled to Brussels, Cologne and Coblenz, where he saw

Ehrenbreitstein, a massive fortification atop a steep cliff rising from the Rhine. It reminded him of Quebec, an association he would reiterate in *Moby-Dick*, referring to Father Mapple's pulpit as both 'his little Quebec' and 'a self-contained stronghold – a lofty Ehrenbreitstein'.[32]

Back in London the second week of December, Melville concluded negotiations with Bentley, who relented and agreed to give him a £200 advance on *White-Jacket*. Bentley's edition would appear the first week of February 1850, receiving lavish praise from the reviewers. One hitherto unrecorded notice from Edinburgh begins with a general assessment of Melville's work:

> Few writers of nautical fiction or narrative have equalled Mr Melville in the graphic delineation of life at sea, of its every-day feelings and occupations, and its thousand marvellous incidents and hairbreadth escapes. Perhaps more than any other writer in the same department he has the power of being minute without becoming tedious. He is equal to all occasions. He can rise with the tempest, and do justice to subjects requiring the exercise of high imagination, and a wild, unwearied, and sprightly humour render him a pleasant and entertaining companion in the dullest weather and amidst even the merest commonplaces of the sailor's existence.[33]

The American edition of *White-Jacket* would appear five weeks after the British edition to largely favourable reviews. Readers were intrigued with the insider's view of life aboard a man-of-war. *Southern Press*, for example, reprinted one chapter, 'Midshipmen Entering the Navy Early'.[34] Caroline Kirkland found *White-Jacket* a 'capital thing', that is, once she could wrest it away from her grown children, who had seized upon the book with avidity. Melville reacted similarly to Kirkland's writings. The previous year he read her *Holidays Abroad* and found its author 'a spirited, sensible, fine woman'.[35]

Castle of Ehrenbreitstein, Coblenz, *c.* 1870, photographic print.

Melville's impassioned critique of flogging in the U.S. Navy attracted many American readers to *White-Jacket*, which fuelled ongoing protests against flogging.[36] A month after its publication Melville's friend J. B. Auld, who had settled in Brooklyn, served on a local committee to abolish flogging in the U.S. Navy. In *White-Jacket* Melville calls flogging 'utterly repugnant to the spirit of our democratic institutions'. The committee's announcement of their organizational meeting echoes Melville's rhetoric: 'All who feel interested in abolishing the brutal and anti republican practice of flogging are invited to attend.'[37]

In September 1850 Congress officially abolished flogging. The Washington correspondent of the London *Morning Chronicle* reported the successful legislation, explaining: 'A great deal of the credit for this act is due to Mr Melville, for the able and graphic manner in which he has depicted the horrors and degradation of the lash, in his *White-Jacket*.'[38]

Before saying goodbye to Bentley in December 1849, Melville coaxed some complimentary books from him – William Beckford's

'Flogging on a Man-of-War', woodcut illustration, from Henry Howe's 24-page abridgement of *White-Jacket* in *Life and Death on the Ocean: A Collection of Extraordinary Adventures in the Form of Personal Narratives Illustrating Life on Board of Merchant Vessels and of Ships of War* (1855).

Vathek, William Godwin's *Caleb Williams*, Mary Shelley's *Frankenstein*. In addition, he purchased copies of Thomas De Quincey's *Confessions of an Opium Eater* and Laurence Sterne's *Tristram Shandy*. Reading De Quincey's *Confessions* the day after buying it, Melville remained by the fire in his Craven Street room, refusing to budge until he finished this 'marvellous book'. Looking at the books he acquired in London, one can almost see *Moby-Dick* – the '*Tristram Shandy* of the sea' – taking shape.[39]

The time Melville spent in London had a profound impact on his ambition and his imagination. On the city's streets and in its dark, smoky taverns the literature of the past lived. London was a place where seventeenth-century folios could still be had, where the shades of James Boswell and Samuel Johnson haunted the side streets branching from the Strand, where the writings of Ben Jonson seemed part of the warp and woof of everyday life. London reminded Melville of a truth his distasteful experiences in the American literary marketplace had obscured: great books last.

No one can walk away from London unchanged. Its influence on Melville is obvious from the direction his work took next. While in London he scouted locations as he researched *Israel Potter*. Leaving the city, he recovered the literary ambitions he had felt during the composition of *Mardi*. His new book would be an epic of whaling, a *King Lear* of the watery world. After returning home in February 1850, he set *Israel Potter* aside and got to work on a book about whaling.

6

Wild Impetuous Grandeur

Though Melville began *Moby-Dick* upon returning from London, he still found time to renew old friendships. The second week of March 1850 he visited Thomas Low Nichols and his wife Mary, who told a friend they had 'a good long visit the other day with Melville' and asked, 'Have you read his *Mardi*?'[1] The New York edition of *White-Jacket* appeared around the same time Melville visited them, *Redburn* four months earlier, but Mary Nichols mentions neither. Instead, she asks about a book that was almost a year old. Her letter implies that *Mardi* formed a topic of conversation during its author's recent visit. A few weeks earlier Melville had presented Evert Duyckinck a copy of the London edition of *Mardi*, hoping the work would find sanctuary at 20 Clinton Place, having otherwise 'been driven forth like a wild, mystic Mormon into shelterless exile'.[2] Of his first five books, *Mardi* best represented Melville's literary ambitions. He kept thinking about *Mardi* in early 1850 because he had recaptured the ambitions it manifested and was now applying them to a new book.

Less than two months after visiting the Nicholses, Melville told Richard Henry Dana Jr that *The Whale*, as he first called *Moby-Dick*, was half finished.[3] His statement seems more wishful thinking than actual fact. A couple days earlier he had borrowed two relevant octavos by William Scoresby from the New York Society Library: *Account of the Arctic Regions* and *Journal of a Voyage to the North Whale Fishery*. Around the same time, Melville visited Putnam's

Richard H. Dana
Jr, 19th-century
wood engraving.

bookstore to order another octavo, the London edition of Thomas
Beale's *Natural History of the Sperm Whale*.[4] He typically acquired
source material at the start of a new project, not halfway through it.

Anticipating an autumn completion date, Melville wrote Bentley
in late June to arrange the London edition.[5] His work on the book
would take a year longer than predicted. The more he wrote the
more his ambitions soared. Ultimately Melville would decide to
do whatever was necessary to make *Moby-Dick* the greatest book
it could be. So far he did not foresee any delays: he had yet to make
the crucial do-whatever-it-takes decision.

His nationwide renown increased with the success of *White-
Jacket*. Sometimes the evidence to verify his reputation takes unusual
form. Two confidence tricksters travelling through the South in 1850
went from town to town offering penmanship lessons. Pretending
to be deaf and dumb, they evoked the sympathy of townsfolk
in Georgia and the Carolinas. Supposedly brothers, they called
themselves 'The Melvilles', one passing himself off as Herman

Melville. Reporting the charade, a North Carolina editor remarked, 'The real Herman will not feel complimented when he learns this.'[6]

In early July Melville felt comfortable enough with his progress on *Moby-Dick* to escape his writer's room. He took the family on vacation to the Berkshires, where they stayed at the old Melvill farm or Broadhall, as it would soon become known. Aunt Mary and her children had recently left Galena and returned to Pittsfield. Since the farm had been sold, they could not stay at Broadhall indefinitely. Returning to Illinois remained a possibility. Unsure where she would end up, Aunt Mary kept her prized possessions close, including the vial of tea from the Boston Tea Party, which she showed to everyone who visited.[7]

That summer Aunt Mary presented Herman with a copy of Nathaniel Hawthorne's *Mosses from an Old Manse*, which represents Melville's introduction to Hawthorne's writings. He briefly returned to New York in late July, inviting Evert Duyckinck and Cornelius Mathews to join him in Pittsfield for a few days. Several other literary figures came together in the Berkshires in the first week of August, including Hawthorne, who was then renting a cottage outside of Lenox, Massachusetts, and Oliver Wendell Holmes, a physician and poet with a summer house near Broadhall.

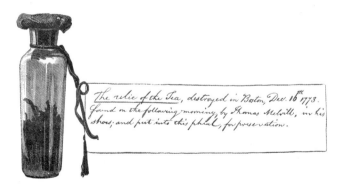

'The Relic of the Tea', engraving from Francis Samuel Drake's *Tea Leaves* (1884).

On 5 August 1850 this motley crew of creative men ascended Monument Mountain. Reaching the top was a challenge for some, but not Melville, the best athlete of the bunch. In an exuberant mood at the summit, he climbed onto a projecting rock resembling a bowsprit and hauled some imaginary ropes to demonstrate something he used to do aboard ship.[8] Dr Holmes reached the summit feeling as though he had dosed himself with ipecac. Hawthorne, who was fifteen years older than Melville, could not quite match steps with him on the incline, but the two stayed in stride at the intellectual level. That day Melville got to know the man behind the book, finding in Hawthorne his soulmate, a fellow writer who understood, truly understood, him in a way that no other writer, no other person, had.

Melville and his guests continued sightseeing for the next few days. On Wednesday he and Elizabeth took Duyckinck and Mathews on a picturesque drive to see the Shakers' settlements and witness their dynamic religious ceremonies in Lebanon. The Shakers offered tourists overnight accommodations. Once Melville found a place to stay, an old Shaker woman showed them to their rooms. Melville noticed an unusual brush with a long handle near one bed and asked what it was for.[9]

'Why I guess it's for him to scratch himself with when he itches,' she replied.

Alive to the local vernacular, alive to every new encounter as he wrote *Moby-Dick*, Melville enjoyed the Shakers and included them in his new book, making Gabriel, the delusional sailor in 'The *Jeroboam*'s Story', a Shaker. Before going to sea, Gabriel had played a prominent role in the Shaker community. During services, he would descend from heaven through a trapdoor, foretelling doom by announcing that he would open the seventh vial, which he carried in his vest-pocket.[10] Gabriel takes all his vials aboard the *Jeroboam*, again threatening to break their seals and bring about total destruction. According to Gabriel, Moby Dick is the Shaker

God incarnate. When Moby Dick kills the first mate, Gabriel interprets the death as a fulfilment of prophecy, effectively terminating the *Jeroboam*'s pursuit of the white whale.

Gabriel's vial in *Moby-Dick* establishes a touchstone for the novel. Ahab carries a vial as a pocket amulet. Filled with sand from Nantucket soundings, Ahab's vial reflects a superstition about magic dirt as protection against evil spirits.[11] Whereas Gabriel's vial can bring destruction, Ahab's supposedly guards against it. Melville thus uses Ahab's vial ironically: it does not protect him at all.

Duyckinck persuaded Melville to write a retrospective review of *Mosses* for the *Literary World*. 'Hawthorne and His Mosses', the best critical appreciation of Hawthorne to appear in his lifetime, also conveys Melville's literary ambitions. Suggesting the possibility that an American author could approach Shakespeare, Melville was not just thinking about Hawthorne, he was thinking about himself.[12] He longed to test out Shakespeare's dramatic devices – soliloquies and stage directions and such – but he was even more anxious to create characters reminiscent of Lear and Macbeth, to capture Shakespeare's humanity. Melville had delayed using Shakespeare extensively in *Redburn* and *White-Jacket*, but *Moby-Dick* let him see whether he could approach Shakespeare in a uniquely American way. He could. He would.

After Duyckinck and Mathews returned to New York, Melville had some quiet time and resumed work on *Moby-Dick*. Discovering his uncle's old desk in the corn loft above the carriage house, he

> found that it was covered with the marks of fowls – quite white with them – eggs had been laid in it – think of that! –
> Is it not typical of those other eggs that authors may be said to lay in their desks, – especially those with pigeon-holes?[13]

Thomas Phillibrown, *Nathaniel Hawthorne*, engraving, 1851.

He cleaned the desk and installed it beneath a window in Broadhall, creating a little nook where he could write with a majestic view of Mount Greylock.

As Melville expanded *Moby-Dick* in sight of the mountain at the farm where he had worked and played in his youth, something extraordinary happened. The book assumed a new and different quality. From a whale-hunting adventure in the South Seas it became a metaphysical journey to the centre of the mind. Revising his manuscript at Broadhall, Melville brought it beyond anything he had so far achieved. It was around this time he made his do-whatever-it-takes decision. In order to make *Moby-Dick* the best book it could be, he decided to leave New York and move to Pittsfield.[14]

Before long Melville found a nearby farm for sale. It had less acreage than the old Melvill place and its ramshackle farmhouse lacked the elegance of Broadhall, but the house had what he wanted most: an upstairs room providing a magnificent view of Mount Greylock. With an infusion of cash from Lemuel Shaw, he put a down payment on the farm, which he named Arrowhead after the relics he found there.

The purchase of Arrowhead manifests Melville's impulsiveness. It made no practical sense. Seated at a desk overlooking a mountain may be an ideal place to write a great book, but when that desk is in a farmhouse requiring countless repairs on a 160-acre farm needing extensive cultivation, quill often yields to hoe and hammer and paintbrush. Transportation was another problem. In New York Melville could walk wherever he wished. Arrowhead was far enough from Pittsfield to require a horse and a vehicle to drive into town, two vehicles really: a three-season buggy and a winter sleigh. Going deep into debt to purchase a place to write *Moby-Dick*, Melville displayed behaviour reminiscent of his father. His aspirations were much loftier, of course. Allan Melvill borrowed heavily to buy fancy French goods to suit the latest fashions; his son borrowed heavily to buy a house where he could write an enduring classic.

Moving from New York to Pittsfield, Melville sacrificed many resources – the New York Society Library, Duyckinck's personal library, Gowans' Bookstore. Pittsfield was not devoid of writerly resources. Local citizens had founded the Pittsfield Library Association earlier that year, but there is no indication Melville used the collection. Forbidding fiction from its shelves, the Pittsfield library contained none of his works.[15]

Having already drafted a basic version of *Moby-Dick*, Melville had less need for sources. The experience of Pierre Glendinning,

Melville's Residence, Arrowhead, Massachusetts.

his greatest tragic protagonist after Captain Ahab, offers a
parallel. An immature author, Pierre has yet to excel his literary
predecessors: he still wants to 'climb Parnassus with a pile of
folios on his back'.[16] Melville himself looked forward to a time
when he could transcend his sources – when 'books no more
are needed for buoys to our souls' – but he had not reached that
point either. He still had the two Scoresby octavos from the New
York Society Library, now grossly overdue, and Beale's *Natural
History of the Sperm Whale* had only just arrived from London the
second week of July. A note Melville inscribed on its title page
verifies that Beale could inspire art: 'Turner's pictures of whalers
were suggested by this book.'[17] Melville may not have had a pile
of folios on his back, but he was trying to scale Parnassus with an
armload of octavos.

In the autumn Herman and his family – wife, son, mother and
sisters Helen, Augusta and Frances – left New York for Arrowhead.
George Duyckinck was sad to see them go. He was quite attached to
the Melvilles and called their home 'one of the pleasantest to visit as
I ever came across'.[18] The move required much hard work and more

time away from *Moby-Dick*, but the breathtaking autumn foliage offered ample compensation.

The first Thanksgiving at Arrowhead was bittersweet. Melville had looked forward to playing host at his new home, but Elizabeth took Malcolm to Beacon Hill for the holiday. Their absence might have given him more freedom to write, but the rest of the family turned his library, the only room at Arrowhead large enough, into a makeshift dining room for Thanksgiving, temporarily depriving him of his workspace.[19]

Thanksgiving dinner turned out well. Aunt Mary and her family came over from Broadhall to enjoy the festivities. After the traditional turkey dinner everyone played fun games, including a fortune-telling game known as 'Home Oracles' that Caroline Gilman had invented.[20] Her *Oracles from the Poets: A Fanciful Diversion for the Drawing-room* contained everything necessary to play the game. Gilman's title page motto extracts lines Macbeth speaks as he implores the witches to reveal their secrets: 'I conjure you, by that which you profess, / (Howe'er you come to know it,) answer me.' The book contains a total of fourteen questions, with sixty possible answers per question, all the answers being extracts from British and American poets.

According to the directions, one person would serve as fortune teller and ask the questions. When asked, the others would choose a number between one and sixty. The fortune teller would then read the passage of verse corresponding to the number. The twelfth question, for example, asks, 'For what have you a distaste or aversion?' If the person asked chose number sixty, the fortune teller would read the following lines from *The Elder Brother*, a Beaumont and Fletcher comedy:

> *Songs and unbaked poetry,*
> Such as the dabblers of our time contrive,
> That has no weight, nor wheel to move the mind,
> Nor indeed nothing but an empty sound.[21]

Though written two centuries earlier, this indictment of contemporary literature seems remarkably appropriate. In Melville's day dabblers still wrote unbaked, empty-sounding verse.

This Thanksgiving the gypsy-eyed Augusta played fortune teller. The first question was for the gentlemen: 'What is your character?' Some of the possible answers were quite critical. Pity the poor gentleman who chose number 27, which repeats what Bassanio says to Gratiano in *The Merchant of Venice:* 'You speak an infinite deal of nothing.' One hopes Herman chose number 24, which excerpts William Wordsworth's *The Excursion*: 'A man thou seem'st of cheerful yesterdays, / And confident tomorrows.'[22]

Few quotations better capture Herman's mood since moving to Arrowhead. All those cheerful yesterdays – his fond memories of life on the Melvill farm with Uncle Thomas and Aunt Mary and Julia and her siblings – were partly what inspired him to buy Arrowhead in the first place. The phrase 'confident tomorrows' reflects Melville's attitude towards *Moby-Dick*. The more he wrote the more his hopes of fame arose. Aware *Moby-Dick* would be a great book, he was confident readers would see it as such, that it would sell enough copies to get him out of debt and let him write more great books.

Melville established a regular routine once he returned to *Moby-Dick* after Thanksgiving. He would get up around eight and go to the barn to feed his horse and cow before having breakfast himself. Afterwards he would go upstairs to his library, light a fire, spread his manuscripts on the table and get to work. He would write until around 2.30 pm, when one of his sisters would knock on the door to announce dinner. He insisted they keep knocking until he answered. Otherwise he would continue to write without eating, without stopping until it got too dark to see. After dinner he would rig his sleigh and drive into town to get the mail. He loved to drive fast, terrorizing whichever female family members dared to accompany him.[23]

Determining when Melville wrote what is a knotty problem. *Moby-Dick* does contain a specific time reference to the period between Thanksgiving and New Year's Day, when Elizabeth and Malcolm would return from Boston. Questioning the controversy over the whalespout's physical nature in 'The Fountain', Ishmael says the issue remains unsolved 'down to this blessed minute (fifteen and a quarter minutes past one o'clock P.M. of this sixteenth day of December, A.D. 1850)'.[24] Melville did not write *Moby-Dick* sequentially. That he was writing the 85th chapter (of a total 135) on 16 December 1850 does not necessarily mean he was nearly two-thirds of the way through the book.

Basically Melville wrote *Moby-Dick* in two stages. He wrote it once and then rewrote it. After his Eureka moment in August 1850, *Moby-Dick*, in Sartre's words, 'came apart at the seams'. Melville realized the novelist's technique was insufficient to tell the story. Sartre continues: 'All means now seemed valid to him: sermons, courtroom oratory, theatrical dialogues, interior monologues, erudition, pseudo-erudition, and the epic.'[25] Within these two major stages of composition, there were several substages. Throughout its composition Melville tinkered with his text, inserting new passages wherever they would fit.[26]

No manuscript of *Moby-Dick* survives, but the partial manuscript of *Typee* and the near-final manuscript of *Billy Budd* together show that Melville's process of composition remained fairly consistent throughout his career. He would write additional text on separate slips of paper and mark his original manuscript to indicate where to insert the added text. One leaf of the *Typee* manuscript, for instance, contains a visual symbol, three dots circumscribed by a diamond. This is no crazy diamond: it designates an additional passage amounting to over seventy words.

Throughout the composition of *Moby-Dick*, the internal evidence suggests Melville expanded his text similarly. Far from interrupting his narrative, all these new interpolations reinforce the inevitability of the novel's action. Maurice Blanchot observes:

> *Moby-Dick* is filled with abysses, summits, detours, twists, and spaces to cross in vain. Enormous abstract digressions brutally interrupt the narrative's course, denying the reader the soothing quality of a straight line . . . Melville wants us to understand that whatever path he follows he cannot go astray. He cannot break the tragic link that joins his heroes to their end.[27]

Melville was writing so much so fast that he ran out of paper in January 1851, when he hitched up his sleigh and took the family to the paper mill in Dalton.[28] With the drive there, the drive back, and a tour of the mill, the excursion turned into an all-day affair. Given the intensity of his creative process, interruptions that took him away from his study typically angered Melville, but this diversion was richly evocative. The female factory workers gave him much to ponder. Paired with memories of a delightful night of masculine camaraderie in London, Melville would reshape their paper mill visit as a diptych, a short-story form he pioneered. He would call it 'The Paradise of Bachelors and the Tartarus of Maids'.

The idea of having Hawthorne nearby was another way Melville justified moving to Arrowhead, but the two seldom saw one another during the composition of *Moby-Dick*. A few times Melville rode his horse to the cottage 6 miles (10 km) away. Hawthorne visited Arrowhead in March 1851 after receiving Melville's irresistible invitation: 'We will have mulled wine with wisdom, and buttered toast with story-telling and crack jokes and bottles from morning till night.'[29] Hawthorne brought with him his adolescent daughter Una, named after the heroine of *The Fairie Queene*. (Melville was not the only one in the neighbourhood with a passion for the poetry of Edmund Spenser.) The sloppy weather prevented Melville and Hawthorne from walking, so they spent their time together

smoking and talking metaphysics in the barn, – Hawthorne
usually lounging upon a carpenter's bench. When he was
leaving, he jocosely declared he would write a report of
their psychological discussions for publication in a
volume to be called *A Week on a Work-Bench in a Barn*.[30]

Having borrowed *A Week on the Concord and Merrimack Rivers*
from Duyckinck the previous year, Melville enjoyed Hawthorne's
joke. Thoreau describes climbing Mount Greylock in his Tuesday
chapter, which reinforced Melville's understanding of the
mountain's literary and cultural significance. Though he would
satirize Thoreau in *The Confidence-Man*, *A Week on the Concord
and Merrimack Rivers* influenced Melville more than he admitted.
Thoreau gave him a model of a wilderness adventure transformed
into a metaphysical journey. Having seen Melville's workspace at
Arrowhead, Hawthorne remembered the image of him writing
Moby-Dick, which he described as 'shaping out the gigantic
conception of his "White Whale", while the gigantic shape of
Greylock looms upon him from his study-window'.[31]

  That spring Melville's farmwork competed with his efforts to
finish *Moby-Dick*. He wanted to fit a modern pump to the well
out back and build a shelter connecting it with the house. He also
needed to smooth out some inconsistencies caused by his extensive
textual revisions. Writing to Hawthorne a few months after he had
visited Arrowhead, Melville explained, 'I have been building some
shanties of houses (connected with the old one) and likewise some
shanties of chapters and essays.'[32]

  'The Lee Shore' is one such shanty chapter. At an earlier stage
of composition Melville had introduced Bulkington, a character
intended as Ishmael's comrade and the book's great truthseeker.
Melville made Bulkington a Virginian but gave him English
roots, naming him after a village in Warwickshire. He would
ultimately split the character in two. Making Queequeg Ishmael's

O. Knirsch, 'The Road, Winter', 1853, lithograph.

companion instead of Bulkington, Melville removed a character
whose name was on every map of England for one whose home,
Ishmael says, is not 'down in any map; true places never are'.[33]
Melville gave Bulkington's predilection for truthseeking to Captain
Ahab. Instead of revising his text to omit Bulkington altogether,
he kept the early references and added 'The Lee Shore' to explain
the character's absence from the rest of the narrative. The chapter
celebrates the willingness to take risks in the pursuit of truth:

> But as in landlessness alone resides the highest truth,
> shoreless, indefinite as God – so, better is it to per-
> ish in that howling infinite, than be ingloriously
> dashed upon the lee, even if that were safety![34]

Omitting Bulkington from the story, Melville developed the
friendship between Ishmael and Queequeg, a South Pacific islander
who has no need for moral improvement. After Queequeg saves a
Nantucket passenger, Ishmael imagines what he is thinking: 'It's
a mutual joint-stock world, in all meridians. We cannibals must

131

help these Christians.'[35] The character of Queequeg is a brilliant technical achievement. Besides letting Melville contrast the assumptions underlying the concepts of savagery and civilization, it let him articulate the theme of male friendship. The intimate scenes depicting Ishmael and Queequeg together constitute some of the most tender moments in American literature. Queequeg also creates many opportunities for humour. After he has locked himself inside their room in 'The Ramadan', Ishmael gets so worried that he breaks down the door in a hilarious scene of physical comedy that anticipates Buster Keaton.

A shanty essay much later in the book opposes 'The Lee Shore'. Separate from the rest of the chapter, the first part of 'A Squeeze of the Hand' has the quality of a late addition.[36] This shanty essay contains the renowned passage in which Ishmael and others plunge their hands into a tub of spermaceti to squeeze out the lumps. The experience creates an ecstatic sense of kindness and fellowship, which lets Ishmael conclude that

> man must eventually lower, or at least shift, his conceit
> of attainable felicity; not placing it anywhere in the
> intellect or the fancy; but in the wife, the heart, the bed,
> the table, the saddle, the fire-side, the country.[37]

Bulkington's landlessness, which symbolizes intellectual pursuit, may lead to the highest truth, but only by abandoning the pursuit of truth, only by lowering expectations, can a person have any chance at happiness. Though Bulkington has disappeared from the narrative, what Ishmael says in 'A Squeeze of the Hand' contrasts with Ahab's pursuit of Moby Dick, which he continues regardless of consequence. Happiness? That means nothing to Ahab.

'Page by page, the story grows until it takes on the dimensions of the cosmos': so Borges said of the composition of *Moby-Dick*.[38] Melville knew he could not keep expanding his book indefinitely.

By early May 1851 he had reached a point where his manuscript was close enough to completion that he could take it to New York to have it set in type and plated: an unusual step. The publisher usually took the responsibility of having a book's stereotype printing plates made. Several possible reasons motivated Melville to take this step – the promise of greater profits, the hope of expediting publication, the opportunity to avoid the straitjacket of a publisher's house style, the ability to control the physical appearance of the finished book – but no reason is more compelling than this: the chance to circumvent an overfastidious editor.[39]

Melville approached Robert Craighead, a 39-year-old printer near the top of his profession.[40] Craighead did not need a complete manuscript in order to start setting a work in type. By initiating production before he had finished writing the book, however, Melville wrote himself into a corner. Putting Pierre Glendinning in a similar situation, he explained the problem:

> Because the printed pages now dictated to the following manuscript, and said to all subsequent thoughts and inventions of Pierre – *Thus and thus; so and so; else an ill match.* Therefore, was his book already limited, bound over, and committed to imperfection, even before it had come to any confirmed form or conclusion at all.[41]

Herman settled into Allan's Manhattan home to finish *Moby-Dick*. When it was nearly complete, he returned to Craighead's printshop in late June, retrieved a bundle of proofs, and left New York for Pittsfield.

Arranging to have *Moby-Dick* plated, Melville also committed himself to overseeing the book's production, something which he had never done before and for which he lacked the temperament. Throughout the composition of *Moby-Dick*, his sisters Helen and Augusta – bless their hearts – had copied his manuscript into a fair copy to submit to the printer. Though experts at deciphering their brother's barely legible hand, they accidentally introduced many transcription errors. Aware there were botches in the work, Melville grew lackadaisical about correcting them when his book was in proofs. He included this aspect of the compositional process in *Pierre*:

> Every evening, after his day's writing was done, the proofs of
> the beginning of his work came home for correction . . . They
> were replete with errors; but preoccupied by the thronging,
> and undiluted, pure imaginings of things, he became impatient
> of such minute, gnat-like torments; he randomly corrected
> the worst, and let the rest go; jeering with himself at the rich
> harvest thus furnished to the entomological critics.[42]

The task of emending the errors that crept into *Moby-Dick* during the book's production has fallen to modern scholarly editors, who have yet to fix them all. An example: Stubb criticizes people whose knowledge of the night sky comes from James Ferguson's *Astronomy*, but the reference became corrupted before publication. The first edition of *Moby-Dick* (and every subsequent one) mentions 'the old women [who] talk *Surgeon*'s Astronomy in the back country'.[43] Melville's modern editors still have work to do.

By summer's end Melville had finished correcting the proofs, which he sent to Allan in New York. In the second week of September Allan forwarded the proofsheets to Bentley to use for the London edition. As Herman's attorney, Allan also signed a contract with the Harpers, which stipulated they publish the book using the plates in Craighead's possession, thus making sure the Harpers would not edit the book and have it replated themselves. Besides saving Herman from possibly having to pay for plating twice, the stipulation guaranteed the integrity of his text.[44] Shortly after Allan signed the contract, Herman changed the title. The change was too late to affect the London edition. Bentley published it as *The Whale*. The Harpers published it under the new title, *Moby-Dick*.

Since Bentley was not beholden to the Craighead plates, he could edit Melville's text as he saw fit. Bentley or the editor he assigned to the task found much to alter. In one scene Queequeg stands his wooden idol up like a bowling pin and invites Ishmael to worship it. Ishmael debates what to do, asking himself:

> Do you suppose now, Ishmael, that the magnanimous God of heaven and earth – pagans and all included – can possibly be jealous of an insignificant bit of black wood? Impossible![45]

Bentley cancelled this passage and numerous others that tread too closely to sacred notions of religion. The meticulous editorial process *The Whale* underwent in London indicates what Melville avoided in New York by having the work stereotyped himself.

Bentley also moved 'Extracts' and 'Etymology' from the front of the book to the back. His editorial staff devoted much thought to their task as they prepared *The Whale* for publication. Sadly, no one at Bentley noticed the absence of the last page of the American proofsheets, which contains the epilogue revealing that Ishmael alone survived the sinking of the *Pequod*. *The Whale* appeared without it. British readers who read the book to its end were shocked to learn they had just read a story told by a first-person narrator who apparently does not survive. Melville's narrative was so daring, so experimental, so groundbreaking that British readers assumed the bizarre denouement was another Melvillean innovation. They had no way to recognize the printing error. Edward Forbes commented, 'How the imaginary writer, who appears to have drowned with the rest, communicated his notes for publication to Mr Bentley is not explained.'[46]

A leading naturalist specializing in marine biology, Forbes also noticed the binding error. Bentley published *The Whale* as a triple-decker or three-volume edition. The spine of each volume was embossed with an image of a right whale, which is the wrong whale. As a naturalist, Forbes also resented Melville's amateurism when it came to his taxonomy of whales. Marine biologists do not typically pause a discussion of, say, the narwhal's horn to insert a piece of bawdy innuendo about Queen Elizabeth, as Ishmael does in 'Cetology': 'An Irish author avers that the Earl of Leicester, on bended knees, did likewise present to her highness another horn, pertaining to a land beast of the unicorn nature.'[47] Forbes's review is not all negative. Parts of *The Whale* he quite liked: 'There are sketches of scenes at sea, of whaling adventures, storms, and ship-life equal to any we have ever met with.'[48]

Some prominent reviewers did not let the erroneous conclusion diminish their enjoyment of *The Whale*. Angus Bethune Reach recognized the power of Melville's imagination and thought *The Whale* his best book yet. It demonstrated Melville's 'almost unparalleled power over the capabilities of the language'.[49] G. H. Lewes singled out 'The Whiteness of the Whale', saying it 'should be read at midnight, alone, with nothing heard but the sounds of the wind moaning without, and the embers falling into the grate within'.[50]

Newly discovered reviews indicate that British appreciation of *The Whale* was even greater than formerly assumed. The London *Daily News* disliked the abrupt conclusion, seeing it as a reflection of the author's contempt toward his readers: 'How the author survives to tell his story is contemptuously left in mystery.' Otherwise the *Daily News* found Melville's work compelling:

> *The Whale* is not the least remarkable work of a very remark-
> able writer. About everything that proceeds from the pen
> of Mr. Melville there is a freshness, an originality, a fascin-
> ation, that nothing can resist. We defy the reader to take
> up one of this writer's fictions, and put it down only *partly*

read. Impossible. He is an ancient mariner, and we are so
many wedding guests. We 'cannot choose but hear'.[51]

The lengthy review the London *Morning Post* published in
November is well known, but the *Post* also published a hitherto
unrecorded early notice. It appeared on 20 October 1851, the same
day as the earliest previously known review of *The Whale*. The
Morning Post notice deserves to be quoted in its entirety:

> *The Whale*, by Herman Melville, just published, is perhaps
> the most extraordinary work that has appeared in England
> for a very great many years. The novelty of the materials that
> constitute the interest – the novelty of the manner of dea-
> ing with them – the poetical, combined with the practical
> nature of the author – the rare power with which he knits
> us to every character in succession – the wild impetuous
> grandeur of his scenes – the impulsive force and vigour of
> his language – these, together, make up one of the most
> fascinating books that was ever read. Captain Ahab is a
> character which few men could have conceived, and how
> few could have drawn with such marvellous earnestness and
> strength; and his pertinacious pursuit of the great white
> whale, Moby Dick, is executed in the true spirit, and with
> the full force of great original genius. Melville is a star,
> and of no ordinary magnitude in the literary firmament.[52]

With profound sadness one turns from the British reviews of *The
Whale* to the American reviews of *Moby-Dick*. *The Independent*, a
Congregationalist weekly, concluded its notice with the following
pronouncement:

> The Judgment day will hold him liable for not turning his
> talents to better account, when, too, both authors and

publishers of injurious books will be conjointly answerable for the influence of those books upon the wide circle of im- mortal minds on which they have written their mark. The book-maker and the book-publisher had better do their work with a view to the trial it must undergo at the bar of God.[53]

Perhaps Melville could laugh off the reviews that appeared in the religious weeklies, but the negative notices in the newspapers and literary magazines wounded him deeply. Evert Duyckinck's review in the *Literary World* hurt the most. Duyckinck was not all negative. Actually he was the first to identify Melville's debt to Goethe, calling Ahab 'the Faust of the quarter-deck' and seeing 'Midnight, Forecastle', as the maritime equivalent of Goethe's Walpurgis Night.[54] But Duyckinck hated having his sacred beliefs questioned. He disliked the scene in which Ishmael kneels down before a pagan idol, but *Moby-Dick* set him on edge from its very start. In his headnote to 'Extracts', Melville introduces the sub-sub-librarian who had supposedly collected all the ensuing extracts. He says that friends who predeceased Sub-Sub were clearing a place for him in heaven 'and making refugees of long-pampered Gabriel, Michael, and Raphael'.[55] Duyckinck could not understand why Melville dislodged these archangels from heaven, commenting, 'We do not like to see what, under any view, must be to the world the most sacred associations of life violated and defaced.'[56] Duyckinck's review disappointed Melville and, within the next few months, would ruin their friendship for years.

Melville knew he had written a great book, a book to last the ages, so all the small-minded critics angered him endlessly. His confidence in *Moby-Dick* had led him to risk everything, to put his family's future in danger for the book's sake. He had been counting on *Moby-Dick* to get him out of debt, pay for the farm, and let him write more books of greatness and ambition. It would not.

7

The Calamities of Authorship

By the time *Moby-Dick* appeared its author had his next book well
underway. Recognizing how intensely Melville worked on *Pierre:
or, The Ambiguities*, V. S. Pritchett remarked: 'He was writing on
one of those waves of hysterical exhaustion that are among the
calamities of authorship.'[1] Between the composition of *Pierre* and
the publication of *The Confidence-Man: His Masquerade* six years
later Melville would undergo many other calamities of authorship,
eventually being forsaken by readers, reviewers and publishers.

The distance between Arrowhead and Manhattan insulated
him from the harshest criticism, and Mount Greylock continued to
inspire Melville, so much so that he dedicated *Pierre* to 'Greylock's
Most Excellent Majesty'. Looking out his window towards the
mountain, he could have been gazing into a mirror. Mount
Greylock was a projection of his inner self, a magnificent landscape
awaiting his exploration. *Pierre*, the finest psychological novel in
American literature before *A Portrait of a Lady*, showed Melville
how perilous the journey into the self could be.

As the novel begins Pierre Glendinning lives in a manor house
with his widowed mother. The sentimentalism of its early chapters
reflects Melville's attempt to write a popular book, but he could not
sustain the tone. It was not in him. The relationship between Pierre
and his mother quickly assumes an undeniable creepiness. She calls
him 'brother'; he calls her 'sister'; and Pierre feels free to enter her
boudoir while she is dressing.

The unnatural intimacy between Mrs Glendinning and her only son warps his sense of male and female relationships. Pierre is engaged to Lucy Tartan, a match his mother approves, but one day a mysterious young woman named Isabel enters his orbit. She identifies herself as his half-sister, whom Mr Glendinning had supposedly fathered outside of wedlock. Isabel's words confirm something about his father's mysterious past that Aunt Dorothea had told Pierre when he was a boy. Melville relates their conversation in a remarkably modern flashback. Aunt Dorothea speaks to her nephew in a stuffy room with the curtains drawn in a scene that anticipates Rosa Coldfield's conversation with Quentin Compson in *Absalom, Absalom!*

Though Isabel offers no definite proof of her genealogy, she convinces Pierre, who feels a bond with her that delves deep into his soul. To explain how Isabel's presence affects Pierre, Melville offers a generalization:

> From without, no wonderful effect is wrought within ourselves, unless some interior, responding wonder meets it. That the starry vault shall surcharge the heart with all rapturous marvelings, is only because we ourselves are greater miracles, and superber trophies than all the stars in universal space.[2]

Melville's language recalls his description of the salt drogher's cabin in *Redburn*. Describing its snug interior as 'a small firmament twinkling with astral radiations', he makes it a world in miniature. In *Pierre* he says that the mind or heart or soul – terms Melville often uses interchangeably – was also a small firmament, one with greater potential for wonder than the heavens above. The mind's extraordinary potential intimidates yet comforts. Though it possesses the vastness of the universe, it can contract into a cosy space. The mind is the mightiest snuggery.

Pierre longs to defend Isabel, to make her a Glendinning and give her the birthright she deserves. What Pierre does not, cannot, admit to himself is that he is strongly attracted to Isabel, who has a mysterious allure Lucy Tartan lacks. His bizarre solution seems doomed to fail. To protect Isabel while keeping secret the daughter whom his father had out of wedlock, Pierre breaks his engagement with Lucy and feigns marriage to Isabel. Mrs Glendinning disowns Pierre, who flees with Isabel to New York, where things go horribly awry.

The best part of *Pierre*, the story of their night-time entry into the city, required Melville to muster all his descriptive powers. He uses chiaroscuro to depict the city in shades of darkness, punctuated by occasional streetlamps that, instead of providing a sense of safety, only darken the shadows, giving evil somewhere to lurk. When his city-dwelling cousin denies him a place to stay, Pierre must leave Isabel at the police watch house for her protection. When he returns, he finds her lost in a sea of pimps and prostitutes, footpads and sneak thieves, drunks and derelicts and all the other malevolent creatures who use the night to mask their menacing activities. To portray them Melville trades his stick of charcoal for a palette of light red and yellow ochre, the colours of blood and plague.

Pierre's urban experience was not unprecedented in Melville's life. When he returned to New York after his trip to Illinois in 1840, he had to reacquaint himself with a changing city. The influx of working-class Irish and German immigrants created a significant demand for low-income housing. Block by block wealthy residents moved uptown, leaving the older buildings in lower Manhattan – warehouses, mansions, churches – to be converted to multifamily residences. Spacious parlours were subdivided into smaller rooms with little regard for light, ventilation or sanitary conditions. Once subdivided, those large old buildings became known as rookeries. 42 Beach Street was one such rookery. Formerly a handsome townhouse located on St John's Square – the city's most beautiful park in Melville's youth – the stately home had since been converted to a boarding house. Melville took a room here in 1840.

Similarly Pierre and Isabel settle at the Church of the Apostles, which has been converted into offices, shops, studios and apartments. The Church of the Apostles anticipates the rookery in Stephen Crane's realist novel *George's Mother*, but Melville was not striving for realism. Pierre Glendinning fits squarely within the Romantic tradition. Inspired by the same predecessors – Shakespeare's Hamlet, Milton's Satan – Pierre resembles such Romantic heroes as Goethe's Faust and Shelley's Prometheus. He dares to challenge anyone and everything – parent, priest, the heavens above – that bar his way.

If the mind could assume the dimensions of the cosmos, it follows that someone who felt such expansiveness might feel a concomitant claustrophobia. Melville had used this idea briefly in *Moby-Dick*. Father Mapple says that Jonah felt 'the little state-room ceiling almost resting on his forehead'.[3] Upon learning about Isabel, Pierre feels a similar sensation:

> He could not stay in his chamber: the house contracted to a nut-shell around him; the walls smote his forehead; bare-headed he rushed from the place, and only in the infinite air, found scope for that boundless expansion of his life.[4]

Pierre's psychological growth reflects that of his creator, who behaved similarly. As *Pierre* neared completion in late December 1851 Melville longed to go outside no matter how blustery the weather. One night he treated himself to a solo sleigh ride. His mother reported: 'On Christmas Eve it was frightfully cold, the wind and snow together blinded every thing. Herman . . . loves to go out in such wild weather.'[5]

Completing what he thought was a near-final version of *Pierre* by year's end, Melville was quite proud of the work – with good reason. In its original form *Pierre* was the most deliberately paced work he had written so far. On or around New Year's Day he left Arrowhead for New York to deliver the manuscript to the Harpers. He stayed with his brother Allan and his family. Isolated at Arrowhead, Herman had not seen too many reviews of *Moby-Dick*, but Allan clipped all those he came across. Melville saw for the first time how negative the American reviews of *Moby-Dick* really were.

The Harpers now questioned Melville's commercial viability. When he followed *Moby-Dick* with a story about a brother and sister living as man and wife and loving as they should not, they were aghast. The theme of brother and sister – two halves of a whole – coming together in search of self-integration had been a prevalent symbol of Romanticism. Think of Manfred and Astarte or Roderick and Madeline Usher. With *Pierre* the Harpers had trouble getting past the literal to the symbolic. Instead of rejecting the manuscript outright, they did something sneaky and underhanded, which shifted responsibility for the book onto its author: they made him an offer so pitiful and demeaning he would be sure to refuse it. Melville needed time to ponder their disappointing offer.[6]

What happened next remains a matter of conjecture. Melville apparently approached Duyckinck for his advice. Though hurt by his review of *Moby-Dick*, Melville still hoped he could rely on their friendship. He was wrong. Duyckinck, too, was aghast. He refused to have anything to do with *Pierre*. He could not, would not, recommend the manuscript to another publisher. He knew no publisher who would touch it. He hoped Melville would abandon the project altogether. If he insisted on publishing *Pierre*, he should take the Harpers' parsimonious offer. Melville went back to the Harpers, accepted their offer, and returned to Allan's house ready to explode.[7]

Ignoring the book's meticulous pace and careful plotting, Melville sabotaged his narrative to vent his spleen. His characteristic impulsiveness and his ability to write quickly proved a dangerous combination. After bringing Pierre and Isabel to New

York, he added a new section making Pierre Glendinning into an author to express his anger and frustration with the whole literary establishment. By the time he finished expanding his manuscript Melville had added 150 pages.[8]

Though the Harpers had committed themselves to publishing *Pierre*, they had not necessarily committed themselves to promoting it. When *Pierre* appeared in the last week of July 1852 the Harpers did little to puff the book. The reviews were few and fierce, with the exception of Oakey Hall's notice in the New Orleans *Commercial Bulletin*. Hall found *Pierre* compelling:

> It is a land story, and barring the air of a seventh heaven of rhetoric, not only interesting, but engrossing. In one great point, it is my *beau ideal* of a novel – at its conclusion, you do not draw a deep sigh, and say, 'Ah, it's all over'; but the book gradually falls from the hand, while in reverie your own imagination upon the author's steed – late rider being dismounted – travels farther and farther on in the regions of speculation.[9]

Sarah Helen Whitman, to name another one of the few appreciative readers, kept thinking about *Pierre* as well. Six years after its publication she could still quote *Pierre* from memory. Visiting Niagara Falls with a friend, she interjected an apt quotation, '"From without", says Herman Melville, "no wonderful effect is wrought within ourselves, – unless some interior, corresponding wonder welcomes it".'[10]

Some reviewers let their dislike of *Pierre* devolve into personal criticism. Several found in the novel evidence that Melville was insane. William Gilmore Simms's comments were among the harshest. 'That Herman Melville has gone "clean daft", is very much to be feared; certainly he has given us a very mad book,' Simms said in his anonymous review. 'The sooner this author is put in a ward the better.'[11]

These accusations of insanity reflect a commonplace belief that writers were more susceptible to mental illness than the general population. Both Byron and Goethe, according to one medical writer, suffered from 'mental idiosyncrasy'.[12] Charles Fenno Hoffman and George Adler followed the stereotype. Committed to the State Hospital in Harrisburg, Pennsylvania, Hoffman would remain there until his death three decades later. Committed to the Bloomingdale Asylum in New Jersey, Adler would be in and out of that institution the rest of his life.

Surveying Melville's career after *Pierre* appeared, Fitz-James O'Brien starkly observed, 'He totters on the edge of a precipice, over which all his hard-earned fame may tumble with such another weight as *Pierre* attached to it.'[13] Melville neither tumbled into the abyss nor went insane. He kept writing. He started a new book, a tale of patience and endurance set on an island off the Massachusetts coast titled *The Isle of the Cross*.

As his work on the manuscript neared completion, Elizabeth gave birth, on 22 May 1853, to their third child, whom they named after her mother and nicknamed Bessie. Priscilla Melvill remarked, 'The *Isle of the Cross* is almost a twin sister of the little one.'[14] Bessie's birth was the third such coincidence. Malcolm had been born on 16 February 1849, around the same time *Mardi* appeared. His younger brother Stanwix had been born on 22 October 1851, the same time Bentley published *The Whale*. The coincidences would continue. Frances, the Melvilles' fourth and final child, would be born on 2 March 1855, a week before *Israel Potter* appeared. Bessie was beset by juvenile arthritis; *The Isle of the Cross* would be stillborn.

Pierre had turned its author into a pariah. When Melville came back to New York and offered *The Isle of the Cross* to the Harpers, they refused the manuscript. London may have been the City of Dis, but New York was the City of Disappointment. Melville could hardly visit without having his literary career assailed in one way or another by critics, publishers and editors. He could not find a publisher for *The Isle of the Cross* and apparently destroyed the manuscript.[15] In light of his inability to publish his latest work, his career as a writer seemed at an end.

George Putnam made it possible for Melville to sustain his literary career. Before Putnam entered the field of periodical publishing, Melville had never considered magazines a suitable outlet for him. Unlike Edgar Allan Poe, who embraced the medium and developed an original aesthetic for magazine fiction, Melville thought great writers should write great books. Short, miscellaneous writing, he believed, dissipated creative energy best channelled into book-length works.

Magazines had never offered authors a livelihood, either. So many people were willing to contribute articles without compensation that most editors and publishers saw no reason to pay authors. Melville had written several reviews for the *Literary World*, but Evert Duyckinck had never paid him for his work. *Harper's Magazine* had published 'The *Town-Ho*'s Story', but the publishers considered the article a promotional pre-publication extract from *Moby-Dick* and did not pay Melville separately for it. The Harpers had other ways to avoid paying contributors for articles. *Harper's Magazine* largely consisted of articles pirated from the British magazines, which saved its publisher from paying or recruiting American authors.

Putnam's emerged as a competitor to *Harper's*. The full title reflects its orientation: *Putnam's Monthly Magazine of American Literature, Science, and Art*. Putting the phrase 'American Literature' in the title, Putnam distinguished the contents of his magazine from the English literature that dominated *Harper's*. To assure the quality of his magazine, Putnam compensated authors fairly. Once the first issue of *Putnam's* appeared in January 1853, *Harper's* sensed a threat and began soliciting contributions from American authors. With his books the Harpers had always charged Melville production costs, refusing to pay royalties until their costs were

'View of Wall Street', 1868, wood engraving.

recouped. The payment system for magazine publication had a neat simplicity: five dollars per page. Melville took advantage of the new opportunity and began writing for both *Putnam's* and *Harper's*.

Though not necessarily the first tale he wrote, 'Bartleby, the Scrivener: A Story of Wall Street' is the first he published. It appeared in two instalments, starting in November 1853 and finishing the next month. According to the magazine's policy, contributions appeared anonymously. Even without Melville's name attached to 'Bartleby', contemporary readers recognized it as a story of great power. One reviewer found it both provocative and exciting.[16]

'Bartleby' takes man's alienation, isolation and unknowability as major themes. The story begins with a traditional motif – the arrival of a mysterious stranger – but it gradually becomes a parable for modern times. The urban setting of 'Bartleby' emphasizes the story's modernity. Set in Wall Street, where the pulse of the nation is measured by the flow of money, the story of Bartleby occurs in an increasingly impersonal and unnatural place. The old lawyer who hires Bartleby and subsequently tells his story has remained in the same office while tall buildings have been erected around him. Bartleby's desk gives him an unobstructed view of a brick wall. His physical situation reflects his psychological state. Working in an office surrounded by tall buildings, he finds himself trapped, walled in by a life he dislikes. Working like a machine, Bartleby has become part of the increasingly mechanized, modernized, regularized world.

Putnam's published several more of Melville's short stories, including 'Benito Cereno', which Edwin Muir calls 'one of his supreme masterpieces, and his most perfect story'.[17] Melville had criticized the practice of slavery in *Mardi*, and the abused and neglected Pip in *Moby-Dick* functions as a commentary on slavery's inhumanity, but 'Benito Cereno', a story of a slave revolt at sea, forms Melville's most extended treatment of the subject. It also offers keen insight into the American national character. With Amasa Delano, who narrates the story, Melville illustrates the ease with which Americans ignore life-threatening danger. The shaving scene, one of the great set pieces in American literature, depicts Babo, the leader of the slave revolt, feigning the role of an obedient slave as he holds a straight razor to Don Benito's throat. Delano does not see through the ruse. Blundering into the danger zone and then blindly escaping from it without learning from his experience, Delano exhibits a pattern of behaviour that would occur time and again over the course of American history.

Depicting the prison where Bartleby spent his final days in 'Bartleby, the Scrivener', 'The Tombs', here shown in an 1874 wood engraving, reflects the Egyptian craze that swept the United States in the early nineteenth century.

In 1855 Putnam sold his magazine to Dix and Edwards. Melville wanted to keep publishing stories in *Putnam's* and also hoped to publish a collection of his short fiction. On a trip to New York in December 1855 he introduced himself to senior partner Joshua A. Dix and pitched the book to him. Melville developed a good working relationship with Dix and Edwards. In 1857 the firm would release *The Confidence-Man*, a complex yet bitter work that exposes the double-dealing hypocrisy endemic to the nation.

Dix saw potential for a short story collection but thought Melville should write a special introduction for it. Initially Melville considered an introduction unnecessary. He saw 'Benito Cereno' as the leading tale and wanted to publish the collection as *Benito Cereno and Other Stories*. On second thought he agreed with Dix and wrote a new piece to introduce the collection. Instead of a conventional introduction, that is, one that overviews the book's contents, Melville wrote 'The Piazza', a work that can stand alone as a separate sketch but also functions as an introduction. Melville reorganized the contents, making 'Bartleby' the first story after 'The Piazza' and placing 'Benito Cereno' after 'Bartleby'. He also changed the title of the volume to *The Piazza Tales*.

Though a fanciful sketch, 'The Piazza' has documentary value. The narrator talks about building a north-facing piazza on his farmhouse; Melville built a north-facing piazza at Arrowhead. The narrator's attitude towards his piazza also reflects Melville's own: 'I like piazzas as somehow combining the coziness of in-doors with the freedom of out-doors.'[18] The piazza is a paradoxical place: an outdoor snuggery.

The narrator's piazza, like Melville's, faces Mount Greylock. Staring at the mountain, he catches a glint of light reflecting from the window of a little cottage, perhaps the home of a fairy princess. One day his curiosity gets the best of him, and he climbs to the cottage, where he meets Marianna, a world-weary young woman. While he has been looking towards her cottage and imagining a better place, she has been looking into the valley and seeing his clapboard farmhouse as a marble palace. Considerately he does not disabuse her of the notion, letting Marianna keep her illusion, the only bright spot in her otherwise dreary life. The narrator returns home wishing he had not wandered off, that he had not let reality displace imagination. In the light of day he can look towards the mountain and recapture his imagination but in the dark his memories of Marianna rush back:

> But every night, when the curtain falls, truth comes
> in with darkness. No light shows from the moun-
> tain. To and fro I walk the piazza deck, haunted by
> Marianna's face, and many as real a story.[19]

Besides leading into them, 'The Piazza' thematically suits the following stories. The theme of loneliness connects all the tales together. The loneliness of Bartleby, a man stranded in a busy city that neither understands nor acknowledges him, differs from the loneliness of Benito Cereno, a man whose sense of racial superiority isolates him as soon as it is challenged. The remaining stories in the collection explore other facets of loneliness. As Muir observes, loneliness occupies Melville's mind, 'a mind passionately resolved to sound its depths and simultaneously to track its curious and erratic windings'.[20]

Reviews of *The Piazza Tales* were largely positive, if not terribly enthusiastic. A Milwaukee reader called 'The Piazza' an 'exquisite word picture . . . worth twice the price of the book'.[21] Few other reviewers spoke as highly. *The Piazza Tales* suffered from DFP (damned with faint praise). The New York *Evening Express* concluded that *The Piazza Tales* 'forms a very pretty parlor volume'.[22] The creator of Captain Ahab and Pierre Glendinning, that is, the creator of tragic heroes with the greatness to rival Lear and Hamlet, had been reduced to writing pretty parlor volumes.

The Melville family recognized what his frustrating literary career was doing to Herman. The intensity of the creative process exhausted him, depriving him of exercise but also draining his psychic powers, which the mediocre critical reception further undermined. Few readers seemed to get him, to understand his works at all. By the time he brought *The Confidence-Man* to a close, he had lost the will, the urge, the energy to write anything. Since borrowing money to purchase Arrowhead, he had been teetering on the brink of financial disaster, often unable to make the interest payments on his loans and sometimes unable to pay the mortgage. He felt like a failure. His grand dreams of becoming a great writer seemed all but over. Happily, his father-in-law rescued him from financial ruin and bankrolled a long recuperative holiday.

Much as Allan Melvill left his family for Europe in 1818 to rebuild his business, Herman Melville left his family for Europe and the Holy Land in 1856 to recover his equanimity. The biggest challenge beforehand was deciding what his family would do in his absence. They chose to shut up Arrowhead. Elizabeth would take Bessie and Fanny with her to Beacon Hill. Herman's sister Helen, who had married two years earlier and moved to Brookline,

Massachusetts, agreed to take Malcolm. After the death of Aunt Catherine – Uncle Herman's wife – in 1855, Maria Melville and her two unmarried daughters, Augusta and Frances, had moved into the old family mansion house in Gansevoort, New York to care for Uncle Herman. They agreed to take Stanwix.

The last week of September 1856 Melville reached New York. He left the manuscript of *The Confidence-Man* with his brother Allan, letting him see it through the press. He also visited some old friends. On the evening of Wednesday 1 October 1856, he went to 20 Clinton Place to see Evert Duyckinck. It had been nearly five years since their friendship fell apart, but they got together that Wednesday as if nothing had happened. They would remain friends until Duyckinck's death in 1878.

Duyckinck's diary entry provides one of the single best records of Melville's personal conversation. It shows he liked to tease Duyckinck but had found a way to bring edgy topics into their conversation without offending his friend's sensibilities. To critique religion or tell dirty jokes Melville need only to couch his subject in literary terms. To discuss atheism, for example, Melville treated it in relation to English literature, arguing that Robert Burton was an atheist and citing some exquisitely ironic passages from *Anatomy of Melancholy*. To interject some bawdy humour, Melville traced it to a literary source. That Wednesday he repeated a story from Boccaccio's *Decameron*. Duyckinck's diary identifies the story Melville told.[23]

Lydia, the beautiful young wife of Nicostratos, a rich old nobleman, was dissatisfied with him and directed her gaze toward Pyrrhus, his handsome young servant. Once she proved her worth, Pyrrhus agreed to sleep with her. She devised a way for them to cuckold Nicostratos before his very eyes. As Lydia sat beneath a pear tree, Pyrrhus climbed it. From his vantage point, he claimed to witness Nicostratos mounting Lydia. Nicostratos told Pyrrhus he was hallucinating. The tree must be enchanted.

For proof Nicostratos climbed the tree himself only to witness Pyrrhus mounting Lydia. Unwilling to acknowledge Lydia's infidelity, Nicostratos concluded that the enchanted tree did induce hallucinations.

The following week Melville and Duyckinck got together with their friend Robert Tomes, who had recently returned from Japan. Melville had seen Tomes in January 1852, when he presented him with a copy of *Moby-Dick*. It is unknown whether the two had got together since then, but Melville kept an eye on Tomes's literary career. The previous year Tomes had published *Panama in 1855*, which Melville added to his Arrowhead library. Duyckinck's diary again provides the evidence for the evening: 'Good talk – Herman warming like an old sailor over the supper.'[24]

Leaving New York on 11 October 1856 Melville reached Glasgow two weeks later. He travelled overland to Liverpool, where Nathaniel Hawthorne was serving as u.s. consul, a position he gained after writing Franklin Pierce's campaign biography. He left an account of Melville's visit in his *English Notebooks*. In Hawthorne's writings Herman Melville is as highly crafted a figure as Roger Malvin. Without necessarily fictionalizing the portrait of his friend, Hawthorne did exercise his powers of discrimination, stressing Melville's melancholy and omitting his humour.

One day they ferried across the Mersey and took the train to Chester, a walled town that looked much the same in Melville's day as it had in Shakespeare's, complete with streets lined by old half-timbered homes. The two friends stopped at a confectioner's to enjoy some veal pies and Bass Ale before touring Chester Cathedral, after which they visited the Yacht Tavern, where Jonathan Swift once stayed. Swift, they learned, had invited the local clergy to dine with him, but none of the reverend gentlemen showed. Swift expressed his anger with an impromptu couplet inscribed onto a windowpane of the tavern with his diamond ring:

Rotten without and mouldering within,
This place and its clergy are all near akin![25]

Hawthorne easily could have transcribed Swift's words into his
journal, but he did not: another indication that he de-emphasized
the humorous elements of Melville's visit to stress his melancholy.

Departing from Liverpool aboard the *Egyptian* on 18 November
1856, Melville sailed through the Strait of Gibraltar, touching at
Algiers and Malta before reaching the Greek island of Syros, from
which he sailed through the Aegean to Thessaloniki and eventually
Constantinople, going from there to Alexandria. After sightseeing
in Egypt, Melville sailed to Jaffa or Joppa, proceeding overland to
Jerusalem, which he reached on 7 January 1857. He allowed himself
plenty of time to explore Jerusalem and its surroundings. When he
returned to Jaffa on 19 January he had difficulty finding a ship. Still
there three days later, he wrote, 'I am the only traveller sojourning
in Joppa. I am emphatically alone, and begin to feel like Jonah.'[26]

The following afternoon Melville ventured to the city's outskirts
to meet Charles and Mary Saunders, American missionaries sent by
the Seventh-day Baptists to convert Jews. Melville mentions them
in his daily account:

Dismal story of their experiments. Might as well attempt to
convert bricks into bride-cake as the Orientals into Christians.
It is against the will of God that the East should be Christianized.[27]

Melville's journal also contains a separate section titled 'Christian
Missions &c in Palestine and Syria'. Though he recognized the
futility of their efforts, this section is nonetheless the most fully
dramatized part of his entire journal, recording a conversation
between Melville and Walter Dickson, another missionary.

One day Saunders accompanied Melville to Dickson's farm
about a half an hour's walk outside Jaffa. Dickson and his family

When Nathaniel Hawthorne was in Liverpool, he enjoyed taking visitors to Chester, England to show them what England had looked like during Shakespeare's time. Unlike so many English cities, Chester still retained many of its half-timbered dwellings, demonstrated by this photomechanical print, *The Cross and Rows, Chester, England*, *c*. 1890.

had left their native Massachusetts for Jaffa two years earlier to teach Jews how to farm before converting them to Christianity. Dickson, an Uncle Sam lookalike, welcomed Melville into his home.

'Have you settled here permanently?' Melville asked Dickson.

'Permanently settled on the soil of Zion,' Dickson replied with a self-satisfied importance that made his wife wince.

'Have you any Jews working with you?'

'No,' Dickson said. 'Can't afford to hire them. Do my own work, with my son. Besides, the Jews are lazy and don't like work.'

'And do you not think that a hindrance to making farmers of them?' Melville asked, unsettled by Dickson's prejudice toward the people he was trying to convert. Melville had encountered the same hypocrisy among the Hawaiian missionaries.

'The Gentile Christians must teach them better,' Dickson replied.

Both Mr and Mrs Dickson asked Melville how their missionary efforts were interpreted back home.

'I can't really answer that,' he replied politely.

Melville's transcript of their conversation soon devolves into a series of etceteras, but he concludes the episode with a sentence characteristic of the author of *The Confidence-Man*: 'The whole thing is half melancholy, half farcical – like all the rest of the world.'[28]

From Jaffa Melville sailed to Athens and then through the Strait of Messina to Naples, from which he took a sidetrip to Pompeii and Mount Vesuvius. He recorded in his journal: 'Pompeii like any other town. Same old humanity. All the same whether one be dead or alive. Pompeii comfortable sermon.'[29] The staccato style of his journal let Melville encapsulate many ideas in few words. Bruce Chatwin offers the best gloss on this journal entry:

> The real lesson of Pompeii, its fascination, the 'comfortable sermon' that Melville heard – is that the human species does not change; that it has a way of surviving catastrophes; and goes on, under the shadow of the Apocalypse, the same venal, bickering, class-ridden, fighting, self-sacrificing, loving, drinking, fornicating species it always was.[30]

After Naples Melville travelled overland to Rome. He visited several other major Italian cities – Pisa, Florence, Venice, Milan, Turin – before heading to Amsterdam and then crossing the English Channel. He reached London on 26 April 1857. After a few anonymous days there he took the train to Oxford. He loved everything about Oxford. Touring the university campus, Melville could see, perhaps for the first time, what his father had denied him when he prevented him from attending college. He also thought about Robert Burton, who used to haunt the Bodleian like a Bartleby.

Louis Haghe, after David Roberts, *Jaffa, Ancient Joppa, April 16th 1839*, 1843, lithograph.

Travelling overland from Oxford to Liverpool, Melville caught a steamer to New York, arriving there on 19 May 1857. Upon his return he decided to sell Arrowhead and move back to New York, though it would take years to unload the farm. He still had no way to earn a living. He had received invitations to lecture since the days of *Typee* and *Omoo* but had always resisted them. Now he took advantage of the opportunity and went on the lecture circuit.

Melville's great storytelling ability did not necessarily transfer to the podium. It could have, but he refused to give audiences what they wanted, which was to hear from the man who had lived among cannibals. Instead Melville cultivated a professorial persona, choosing to lecture on Roman statuary for the 1857–8 season. He wrote out his lecture and read it, seldom making eye contact or engaging with the audience. He chose a more amenable topic for the next lecture season, 'The South Seas', but had little more success. He wrote a new lecture for the 1859–60 season, but made only a few appearances before abandoning the lecture circuit altogether. Once again Melville found himself without the means to support his family.

Judge Shaw had rescued his son-in-law several times already, but Melville could not rely on him indefinitely. On Saturday, 30 March 1861, Lemuel Shaw quietly passed away in his Beacon Hill home. Shaw's devotion to his only daughter provides one reason why he kept coming to Melville's rescue, but there is another way to explain his devotion to the Melville family. When Shaw's personal effects were examined after his death, his wallet was found to contain two letters from Herman's Aunt Nancy, dating from 1813. Through 48 years and two marriages, he had kept the last letters of his first love close to his heart.[31]

A third explanation for Judge Shaw's support involves his respect for Melville as an author. Though he sometimes disagreed with what Melville wrote, Shaw admired his son-in-law's willingness to publish his ideas. Judges and authors share a crucial similarity. Both are public figures. As chief justice of Massachusetts, Shaw often made controversial decisions and expressed unpopular opinions. Like his forward-thinking son-in-law, he said things that rattled people's beliefs. Shaw understood that authors also exposed themselves to public censure. He knew the only way for a person to avoid censure would be to say nothing, to do nothing, and he had no respect for people who were too meek to open their mouths in public.

Shaw's death meant the death of Herman's greatest supporter in the Shaw family. Neither his second wife nor her two sons liked Herman, but Shaw refused to let them badmouth him. After Shaw's death they freely expressed their animosity towards Herman. Elizabeth also felt free to criticize her husband after her father's death. She told her stepmother and stepbrothers that Herman was going insane, a claim based on her superficial knowledge of mental illness. Elizabeth accepted both the stereotype of the writer's susceptibility to mental illness and the idea that insanity could be hereditary. Hadn't Herman's father raved from his deathbed? After

Shaw's death his widow and their two sons encouraged Elizabeth to leave her husband.

The whole situation sounds like a fractured fairy tale: once upon a time Cinderella's evil stepmother and her two evil stepbrothers encouraged her to flee Prince Charming. The parallel quickly breaks down. Elizabeth was no Cinderella, Herman no Prince Charming. Despite her family's encouragement, Elizabeth never left Herman, though the two did spend more time apart, her seasonal allergies providing the perfect excuse for her to escape to the White Mountains for weeks or months at a stretch.

Once Elizabeth received a portion of her inheritance, the Melvilles could afford to rent a house in New York City in early 1862. That summer they returned to Arrowhead, mainly to get it ready for sale. Herman's brother Allan agreed to purchase it as a summer house. Herman and Elizabeth bought his former home on East 26th Street, though Allan took advantage of Elizabeth, forcing her to take out a mortgage on the difference. After thirteen years in the Berkshires, Herman Melville, the New York native, was coming home. 104 East 26th Street would be the Melvilles' address for the rest of Herman's life.

8

The Modern Ossian

Once inside the gnarly defensive perimeter the Union troops
constructed at Vienna, Virginia, Melville could view the Civil
War from the soldier's perspective, something he considered
essential to the latest phase of his literary career. He had decided
to remake himself into a modern-day Ossian. Written by James
Macpherson, inspired by traditional Gaelic verse, and attributed
to a legendary Scottish bard, the Ossianic prose poems developed a
large following in the late eighteenth and early nineteenth century.
Macpherson's Ossianic collections stress the bard's importance on
the battlefield. Fallen heroes need someone to sing their praises.
Macpherson made the poet as essential to the battlefield as the
warrior. Proud of the military exploits of both his grandfathers,
Melville also wanted to make his mark on the battlefield. A 41-year-
old father of four suffering from sciatica when the Civil War broke
out, Melville lacked the stuff to be a soldier, but he could achieve
a lasting place in the history of the Civil War by chronicling it in
verse.

Melville had started writing poetry before the war. In 1860
he drafted a book-length collection of verse but failed to find
a publisher. He remained undaunted. In the early 1860s he
embarked on a rigorous programme of study, reading poetry from
throughout the history of English verse. Precisely when he decided
to chronicle the war in verse is unknown. In an introductory note

to *Battle-Pieces and Aspects of War*, as he would title his collection of Civil War poetry, Melville says the fall of Richmond inspired him to prepare the volume, but he had begun to identify with Ossian long before Richmond fell in April 1865. He read Macpherson's Ossianic verse so thoroughly that he could make comments about it as a whole. When, in 1862, he read William Hazlitt's remark that Ossian 'was without God in the world', Melville inscribed the following note in the adjacent margin: 'True: no gods, I think, are mentioned in Ossian.'[1] Melville clearly appreciated Macpherson's ability to express the bloodshed of the battlefield without recourse to divinity.

He reached Vienna on 16 April 1864. The camp there had been established mainly to counter the activities of John Singleton Mosby, commander of the 43rd Virginia Partisan Ranger Battalion. For months Mosby had been conducting guerrilla operations in northern Virginia, raiding enemy supply lines, seizing federal arms and ammunition, and capturing enemy troops. Colonel Charles Russell Lowell, commander of the 2nd Massachusetts Volunteer Cavalry Regiment, faced a difficult mission: stop Mosby.

Colonel Lowell impressed Melville. Well educated and well read, Lowell could talk books with the literary celebrity in his camp. Having learned that Mosby's men were near Leesburg a few days earlier, Lowell planned a reconnaissance operation to Aldie, Virginia, to search for them. He would send the infantry west and then ride with the cavalry to rendezvous with the infantry at a picketed camp outside Aldie. When Lowell invited him to accompany the cavalry, Melville accepted. Borrowing a horse, a saddle and some warm clothing, Melville was ready to ride.[2]

When the bugler sounded 'Boots and Saddles' the morning of 18 April, Melville mounted his steed and joined the scouting party. Lowell led the column, keeping his distinguished guest close. After riding all day, they bivouacked on the road. Melville experienced at first hand the difficult conditions cavalrymen faced during the war.

Since they had to be ready to ride at a moment's notice, they could not unsaddle their horses that night. Melville, like the other men, had to lie on the ground next to where his horse stood. If that were insufficient to prevent sleep, enemy signal rockets lit up the night sky and Mosby's rangers shot at Union pickets.[3]

Lowell sent out search parties the next morning. The largest group captured eleven rangers, including an officer. Melville listened to the prisoners to learn their speech rhythms, a carryover skill from his novel-writing days. Lowell received intelligence that a ranger was getting married in Leesburg that evening and that Mosby was supposed to attend the wedding. In retrospect the intelligence seems planted. Throughout their scout towards Aldie, Mosby shadowed the Union cavalry, keeping abreast of every move.[4]

That afternoon the cavalry joined the picketed infantry outside Aldie. Lowell sent a 75-man force into Leesburg. When the Union soldiers reached the hotel where the wedding was scheduled, the crowd was dispersing. Aware that Union troops might appear, the wedding guests came well armed. A brief skirmish left two Union soldiers dead and three wounded. The Union forces returned to the camp outside Aldie late that evening.[5] The cavalrymen broke camp the next morning and headed back towards Vienna. As they approached, the military band played celebratory music, which sounded somewhat inappropriate to sensitive ears. A mission that left two Union soldiers dead and Mosby at large hardly seemed like something to celebrate.

Melville's participation in the reconnaissance mission inspired the longest poem in *Battle-Pieces*, 'The Scout toward Aldie'. In rough outline the poem follows the journey he took with the cavalry, but Melville strayed from reality as he reshaped events into a literary ballad. He simplified the action, omitting the infantry altogether. Though based on Lowell, the colonel in the poem is more brash and headstrong than the cool and calculating original.

Headquarters of Lowell's Cavalry Brigade, Vienna, Virginia, February 1864.

And Mosby became more symbol than man. Besides being a brilliant military strategist, the real Mosby was a sophisticated man of law and letters. In the poem he is a mysterious and malevolent force. Each stanza ends with a couplet, and each couplet makes reference to Mosby. The speaker of the poem repeats the name 'Mosby' to intensify the poem's sense of fear and foreboding.

Though Melville partly fictionalized the journey, he hardly needed to alter the landscape. Some details, though realistic, lend a fantastic quality to the poem's setting. Consider the fifth stanza:

> They lived as in the Eerie Land –
> The fire-flies showed with fairy gleam;
> And yet from pine-tops one might ken
> The Capitol Dome – hazy – sublime –
> A vision breaking on a dream:
> So strange it was that Mosby's men
> Should dare to prowl where the Dome was seen.[6]

Col. John S. Mosby, CSA, photograph, c. 1860.

April was too early for fireflies, but Melville never gave the poem a specific time setting. When the fireflies came out that summer Mosby was still leading guerrilla raids in northern Virginia. Whereas Coleridge had to imagine a stately pleasure dome for 'Kubla Khan', Melville had a real dome he could put in 'The Scout toward Aldie'. The newly erected dome of the u.s. Capitol towered over the landscape. Melville used the realistic details to create a fantastic yet ironic landscape: the Civil War was partly fought within view of a great symbol of national unity.

Battle-Pieces owes a debt to Macpherson's Ossianic verse not only in terms of its general purpose but for some of its specific imagery. 'The Armies of the Wilderness' echoes 'Carthon', one of Macpherson's most popular prose-poems. In this poem Fingal laments the destruction of Balclutha, a walled town belonging to the Britons. With Ossian's popularity Balclutha became a symbol of desolation. Melville appreciated Charles Lamb's use of Balclutha to describe the South Sea House and highlighted the corresponding description in his copy of *Fingal*, one of Macpherson's Ossianic collections:

I have seen the walls of Balclutha, but they were desolate. The fire had resounded in the halls; and the voice of the people is no more. The stream of Clutha was removed from its place, by the fall of the walls. – The thistle shook, there, its lonely head: the moss whistled to the wind. The fox looked out, from the windows, the rank grass of the wall waved round his head.[7]

Melville borrowed imagery from 'Carthon' for 'The Armies of the Wilderness', depicting how the deserted military camps would appear in the last days of the war:

The weed shall choke the lowly door,
And foxes peer within the gloom,

> Till scared perchance by Mosby's prowling men,
> Who ride in the rear of doom.[8]

As in 'The Scout toward Aldie', Mosby's men in 'The Armies of the Wilderness' are not men. They are ghoulish reminders of the ubiquity of evil.

Published in August 1866 *Battle-Pieces* received fainter praise than *The Piazza Tales*. A few readers appreciated the whole volume. The reviewer for the *Indianapolis Daily Journal*, for one, thoroughly enjoyed it:

> We have often wondered why Herman Melville did not write poetry. The volume before us shows that he does write it, and that of the best quality. The battle pieces have the true martial ring. They are swift in movement, stirring in tone, and vividly suggestive of shot, shell, sabre stroke, and garments rolled in blood. 'Sheridan at Cedar Creek' is a lyric unsurpassed; and this is but representative of the excellences manifested throughout the work.[9]

Few other reviewers were as positive, but almost everybody loved 'Sheridan at Cedar Creek'. One reader considered it the best cavalry poem in the English language after Robert Browning's 'How They Brought the Good News from Ghent to Aix'.[10]

Battle-Pieces had little impact on Melville's life. After its publication he resumed his search for a government appointment. Before year's end he received an offer from the New York Custom House, which he accepted. Starting the first week of January 1867, Herman Melville became U.S. Customs Inspector No. 75.

He was not the only literary man working for U.S. Customs. Richard Grant White did, too. Though White lacked the talent and ambition to be a great writer, he had tried to make a living in the world of letters. He had written a life of Shakespeare, contributed dozens of articles to the magazines, and edited several books. The year Melville published *Battle-Pieces*, White compiled an anthology, *Poetry, Lyrical, Narrative and Satirical, of the Civil War*. Unable to earn a living with his pen, White had turned to the U.S. Customs Service.

After work Melville and White sometimes visited A. L. Luyster's Bookstore, 138 Fulton Street. With 'a vast collection of volumes lining the walls of several large rooms in the upper part of the spacious building', Luyster's shop appealed to both men. Another customer remembered seeing Melville there:

> In the flesh he did not show either strength or determin-
> ation; on the contrary, he was the quietest, meekest,
> modestest, retiringest man you can imagine. He moved
> from shelf to shelf so quietly – I never saw him speak to
> anyone – and his air was that of shrinking timidity.[11]

Luyster's Bookstore was not the only one Melville patronized in his waning decades. Oscar Wegelin, who apprenticed at Anderson's Bookstore, remembered that Melville 'walked with a rapid stride and almost sprightly gait' and recalled 'his gentleness of manner and his pleasant smile'.[12]

Through the final third of the nineteenth century the Civil War remained prominent in the national memory. Whereas those who fought in the war increasingly romanticized their exploits, those born after the war – think Stephen Crane – saw little to romanticize. Perhaps those born beforehand but too recently to serve had the hardest time coming to terms with the war. Aged twelve when the Civil War began, Malcolm Melville, like many boys his age, felt he had lost the chance to prove himself in the crucible of war. With two Revolutionary War heroes as great-grandfathers, Malcolm sensed the loss more acutely than others.

Richard Grant White, photograph, *c.* 1860.

To compensate Malcolm joined a volunteer regiment with others his age. They took pride in their uniforms and their sidearms. Malcolm's regiment gave him a sense of belonging but did not fulfil all his psychological needs. On the evening of 10 September 1867 he stayed out until the small hours and apparently slept in the next day. When his father came home from work he found the door to Malcolm's room still locked. In a tragic re-enactment of the comic scene from *Moby-Dick*, Melville broke down the bedroom door to discover that Malcolm had shot and killed himself.

A coroner's inquest called his death a suicide. Malcolm died 'by shooting himself in the head with a pistol . . . while laboring under temporary insanity of mind'.[13] The verdict raised the spectre of inherited insanity, but the family denied the coroner's findings altogether. The Melvilles insisted the shooting was an accident. Uncle Peter's daughter Kate Gansevoort, who was becoming increasingly important to them, empathized with the Melvilles. 'I pity the poor parents,' she said. 'Both Cousin Herman and Lizzie are of such nervous temperaments I should fear for *their peace of mind*.'[14]

Though his job as customs inspector occupied much of Melville's time, he still enjoyed walking around the city. Sometimes he ran into reminders of his family's past. While on his lunchbreak from work one day in 1870 he visited the Gansevoort Hotel, where he bought some tobacco to initiate a conversation.[15]

'Can you tell me what this word "Gansevoort" means?' Melville asked the man serving him. 'Is it the name of a man? And if so, who was this Gansevoort?'

That man did not have an immediate answer, but another within earshot overhead Melville's questions and offered an answer.

'Sir', the other man said, catching Melville's attention. 'This hotel and the street of the same name are called after a very rich family who in old times owned a great deal of property hereabouts.'

The man's ignorance stunned Melville. He could hardly believe the hero of Fort Stanwix had been so completely forgotten. Instead of correcting him, Melville left the hotel in a huff and returned to his office, where he 'moralized upon the instability of human glory and the evanescence of – many other things'.[16]

His sister Helen had a happier experience a few years later. The date 16 December 1873 marked the centenary of the Boston Tea Party. The City of Boston celebrated in grand style at Faneuil Hall. As a granddaughter of Major Thomas Melvill, Helen attended the event. Aunt Mary loaned the precious vial of tea to the occasion. After making a not-very-clever comparison between casting bread upon the waters and casting tea into Boston Harbor, the Reverend Edward Everett Hale held up the vial and showed everyone the tea Major Melvill had carried home in his boots that fateful night a hundred years earlier.[17]

Melville continued reading poetry outside of work. His reading eventually inspired him to embark on an ambitious, book-length poem. The full-time job at the Custom House prevented him from immersing himself in the project as he had with *Moby-Dick*, but he adopted a new writing process, adding a few lines of verse whenever he had the time. The result would be *Clarel: A Poem and a Pilgrimage in the Holy Land* (1876), a narrative poem in irregularly rhyming iambic tetrameter that runs to nearly five hundred pages in the modern edition.

Fifty years after *Clarel* appeared John Freeman remarked, 'Descriptive verse is no longer in vogue . . . as to a large part of *Clarel*'s purpose, it is fulfilled more admirably by the cinema.'[18] Long narrative poems were already out of fashion when Melville published *Clarel* in 1876. His metre was reactionary, being the same Sir Walter Scott had used for his descriptive verse. In terms of Melville's own work, *Clarel* recalls *Mardi* more than anything. Like Taji, Clarel passively observes the characters he encounters but possesses little personality himself. Why did Melville write *Clarel*?

Perhaps that question is not too difficult to answer. Melville's career path follows that of great writers, not popular ones. Popular authors seldom venture beyond the pattern their first best-seller establishes. Following a successful formula, they create a set of expectations for readers and then satisfy them (the expectations and the readers). Great writers, alternatively, challenge reader expectations. Melville's career could have gone either way. He established a successful formula with *Typee*, which he closely followed in *Omoo*. Speaking of his early success, Walker Percy called Melville 'a sort of Louis L'Amour of the South Seas'.[19] But Melville refused to keep following the formula. Instead he pushed himself, taking his art beyond anything he had written previously. Having demonstrated what he could do in prose, he extended his literary reach with poetry. *Battle-Pieces* was a kind of sampler in which Melville wrote many different types of verse to demonstrate what he could do. Despite the time he spent writing short stories in the 1850s, he still believed that great writers should write great books. Whatever his other shortcomings Melville was never short on ambition. He conceived *Clarel* as a great book, an epic poem to rival *Paradise Lost*.

Robert Browning, one of the most important influences on Melville's poetry, believed that readers should have to work hard to understand his verse. Melville agreed. *Clarel* is an extremely challenging work that demands time and patience. Richly detailed yet paradoxically elliptical, *Clarel* requires readers to linger over every line. Entire books have been written about *Clarel* without exhausting its interpretive possibilities.[20] For now a single excerpt must suffice. Near the end of *Clarel* Melville offers a final picture of Jerusalem, showing how it appears at night:

> The valley slept –
> Obscure, in monitory dream
> Oppressive, roofed with awful skies
> Whose stars like silver nail-heads gleam
> Which stud some lid over lifeless eyes.[21]

Besides reusing imagery from his fiction, this passage also recalls Ossianic verse, which frequently parallels dwelling place and sepulchre: Ossian's favourite term for the grave is the 'narrow house'. Previously Melville had contrasted small, enclosed spaces with the expansiveness of the star-studded heavens above. He reuses the same imagery here, but now all those astral radiations, formerly symbols of majesty and wonder, are so many coffin nails. Figured as a dead city, Jerusalem is blind to the stars above.

As *Clarel* neared completion, Melville devoted his efforts outside the Custom House to the poem. His daughter Fanny remembered him waking her after midnight to correct proofs. During the late stages of *Clarel*, Elizabeth, with some trepidation, could see Herman slipping into the same pattern of behaviour he had demonstrated at the peak of his career 25 years earlier. She looked forward to the book's publication, which, she hoped, would improve his physical and mental well-being.[22]

Clarel appeared the month before the nation celebrated its hundredth anniversary on 4 July 1876. Filled with scepticism and uncertainty, *Clarel* offered an ironic comment on the U.S. Centennial. It attracted little attention and scarcely affected Melville's daily life. He kept going to work at the Custom House six days a week. The fact that Chaucer, the author of another great long poem, had worked at the Custom House in his day offered small consolation.

Melville's job only allowed him two weeks' vacation, but Elizabeth and their daughters had started taking longer vacations, leaving Herman in New York to keep bachelor's hall. Given its limited duration, his summer holiday was typically quite hectic. The year after *Clarel*'s publication, he visited Albany the second week of August to see Kate Gansevoort or, properly, Kate Gansevoort Lansing. Four years earlier she had finally married her cousin and best friend Abraham Lansing. Melville also went to Gansevoort, New York, where his sister Frances continued to live in the increasingly decrepit mansion house since the deaths of their mother and sister Augusta. After seeing Frances, Herman continued to Jefferson Hill, New Hampshire, to join his family in the White Mountains.

The leading travel guide shows why Jefferson Hill appealed to Elizabeth: 'Sufferers from hay-fever and catarrhal complaints receive relief here.'[23] The tremendous view appealed to Herman. The Plaisted House, the hotel where they stayed in 1877, had a wrap-around piazza, offering an astounding view of the Presidentials: Mount Adams, Mount Jefferson and Mount Washington could all be seen from the Plaisted piazza.

Henry B. Thomas also stayed at the Plaisted House that summer. Thomas – Harry to his friends – was in the hotel lobby buying a cigar when Melville entered to do the same. The two had never met before, but Melville quite impressed the young man. Thomas recalled: 'He came into the lobby to buy a cigar. He did it with a certain air. I did not know who he was, but he bought a cigar and walked out in a way that impressed me.'[24]

Herman was not the only Melville to catch Thomas's attention that summer. Fanny Melville, now 22, also caught his fancy. They spent much time together in New Hampshire, and, after the Melvilles returned to New York, Thomas visited.[25] The first night he stopped by 26th Street, Harry could hardly tear himself away. As he and Fanny sat together in the front parlour late into the night, her father decided that Thomas had overstayed his welcome. He stormed down the hallway towards the parlour.

'Young man,' Melville yelled. 'Do you prefer oatmeal or mush for breakfast?'

Thomas got the message and quickly said his goodbyes. Fanny was furious. She worried he would never come back. She need not have. Harry had plenty more opportunities to enjoy oatmeal with the author of *Omoo*, an autodidact of the breakfast table. By the following Easter, the couple had become engaged.

Herman Melville, etching after portrait by Joseph Eaton, pre-1891.

Their engagement would last the next two years, time enough for Melville to put his potential son-in-law through his paces. Despite his increasingly pessimistic outlook, Melville had never lost the playfulness that had been part of his make-up since childhood. One day he served crab for dinner. With board and hammer before him, Melville cracked jokes as he cracked crab. His behaviour amused Harry but infuriated Fanny. When Harry retold the story to his family in the coming years, Fanny would roll her eyes and sigh.[26]

On 5 April 1880 Harry Thomas and Fanny Melville were married in Manhattan at All Souls Church. They settled in East Orange, New Jersey, a ferry-and-train ride away from 26th Street.

Harry Thomas became good friends with his father-in-law, and his reminiscences provide some of the best information about Melville's later years. Thomas explained how Melville made time for writing while still working full time. Typically he worked from early morning until one or two in the afternoon, when he would come home for dinner. After dinner Melville would 'shut himself up in his room, and no one knew or dared inquire as to what busied him there'.[27] Neither Thomas nor anyone else could get Melville to discuss what he wrote: 'He never talked about his writing . . . If anyone brought up the subject, he'd shut up like a clam.' Melville was more than happy to discuss other topics. Thomas continued:

> He talked freely and most interestingly on many subjects not connected with his books. He was fond of walks in the country and liked to talk about nature. I remember many interesting talks on politics and religion. He was very much down on politicians. He called them 'damn fools'. In fact, that was the term he applied to nearly everybody. He wasn't sociable, you know. He didn't care for people.[28]

The Thomases settled into a comfortable life in East Orange. Fanny gave birth to Eleanor, their first child, on 24 February 1882. Frances, their second daughter, was born on 3 December 1883. Fanny would give birth to two more daughters, but she also became active in the community. She, too, felt the impact of her great-grandfathers and joined the Essex County branch of the Daughters of the American Revolution.[29]

Melville occasionally visited East Orange to see his grand-daughters. Eleanor would become a Melville scholar. Her book, *Herman Melville: Cycle and Epicycle*, presents many important family documents that shed light into the darkened corners of Melville's life. His granddaughters, along with a few other children he met late in life, left better anecdotes about Melville than the members of his own generation.

Like Melville, Thomas was an excellent athlete. In the mid-1880s no sport appealed to adventuresome young gentlemen more than bicycling. By the summer of 1886 Harry Thomas had purchased a high-wheeled bicycle of his own.[30] That August, as Fanny told her father, Harry took a bicycle tour from New Jersey to Pittsfield, an ambitious 350-mile (560-km) round trip that followed some excellent roads through the Housatonic Valley and took the better part of a week to complete. He was also an active member of the local cycling club, the Orange Wanderers – 'very active', according to club president L. H. Porter. The next year Thomas was elected vice president of the Orange Wanderers.[31]

The final third of the nineteenth century was the golden age of the American club, a time when some of the finest clubs in the nation were established. The Orange Wanderers was not Thomas's only club. He was also a founding member of the Orange Athletic Club and served as its first secretary. The clubhouse, which opened in 1887, housed two full-sized tennis courts, a gymnasium, a four-lane bowling alley, a billiard room and a reading room. The club fielded its own amateur football team, which competed against the likes of Rutgers and Princeton.[32]

Harry Thomas took great pride in the Orange Athletic Club and, presumably, invited his father-in-law to enjoy it, but there is no proof Melville ever visited the club. He had several friends and relations who were clubmen and received many similar invitations, nearly all of which he refused. Melville's physician Everett S. Warner, for one, was an active member of the Berkeley Athletic Club of New York. When Abraham Lansing invited Melville to the Fort Orange Club in Albany, he turned him down, calling himself an old fogey.[33]

While refusing invitations to visit some clubs and join others, Melville imagined a club all his own, the Burgundy Club. With Major John Gentian, his ideal clubman, Melville extended his literary use of the Civil War. A war hero who lost an arm in combat, Major Gentian is a superb storyteller. Told within the confines of a private club, his war stories are narratives shared solely between teller and listener. Unlike written works, they are subjected to neither the scrutiny of narrow-minded critics nor the judgement of a fickle public. The Burgundy Club offered Melville a distinct advantage over real clubs. He could imagine conviviality while preserving his solitude, an impulse that was increasingly precious to him.[34]

The Burgundy Club sketches grew out of headnotes Melville wrote for some of his poems. They represent his first prose fiction since *The Confidence-Man*. More than anything, they resemble the *Spectator* essays of the previous century, Major Gentian performing a similar role in the Burgundy Club sketches that Sir Roger de Coverley plays in the *Spectator* essays. Fitz-James O'Brien had recommended that the author of *Pierre* 'diet himself for a year or two on Addison'.[35] It took three decades, but Melville had finally taken O'Brien's advice. Ossian had given way to Addison, and the Burgundy Club sketches cleared the way for Melville's last great work, *Billy Budd*.

Retiring from his post as customs inspector at the end of 1885, after nineteen years' service, Melville could return to writing full time, but 1886 had hardly begun before tragedy struck. Stanwix, the Melvilles' second son, had always been restless. He read law, studied dentistry and worked as a sheep farmer, travelling to China and Nicaragua, Kansas and California. By the start of 1886 he was living in San Francisco and suffering from tuberculosis. He succumbed to the disease on 23 February 1886. He was 34.

When the Thomases showed up at 26th Street one day, Elizabeth Melville saw that Fanny had dressed her daughters with black hair ribbons. Elizabeth refused to let her granddaughters wear mourning and traded their black ribbons for brightly coloured ones.[36] It did seem as though hardly a year went by that decade without another death in the family. Aunt Mary had died in 1884, the same year as Herman's youngest brother Tom, and their sister Frances died in 1885. Frances's death meant that the family would close up the mansion house in Gansevoort. Herman's sister Helen oversaw the task of packing up all the family furniture and shipping the pieces to whomever Frances had bequeathed them.[37]

In the summer of 1886 Herman reached Gansevoort amid the hurly-burly of packing. Worthless at such tasks, he borrowed a horse and buggy and drove to Glens Falls to get a haircut from a barber he liked. Ferris Greenslet, a local boy who happened to visit the barber the same time, left what is arguably the best Melville anecdote of all. At eleven Greenslet was just the right age to view the world of adults with wonder, the age to learn that grown-up talk was different from kid talk, that a man's private parts were not always something to whisper and titter about, that there were valid and very practical reasons to discuss the subject. A tailor, for example, needed to know whether a man 'dressed right' or 'dressed left', simple facts of inherited anatomy. Barbershop talk awakened Greenslet to this adult world. Subsequently an editor at Houghton Mifflin, he had an excellent memory for detail and recalled many aspects of his boyhood in his autobiography.

Greenslet omitted the barbershop episode from his autobiography but related it privately and swore to its veracity.[38]

'Tell us some more about those adventures you had in the South Seas,' the barber said, egging Melville on.

In response Melville initiated what Greenslet called a 'flow of joyous narrative'.

'Weren't there any girls down there?' the barber asked.

'I'll say there were! I went back to the island a couple years after I left there on board a man-of-war,' Melville explained. 'The first thing I saw when I went ashore was my own little son about a year and half old running around naked in the sun on the beach.'

'How did you know it was your son?' the barber asked.

'He had to be,' Melville replied. 'He carried his bowsprit to starboard!'

Remarkably Greenslet was not the only child who met Melville in 1886 and left a vivid anecdote of his conversation. That summer Melville visited Albany to see the Lansings. Anna Pruyn and her adolescent daughter Huybertie stopped by when he was there. Like Greenslet, Huybertie Pruyn had an excellent memory and wrote an autobiography of her childhood. Her autobiography briefly mentions Melville, but she described him in fuller detail to an Albany reporter.[39]

Once Anna Pruyn and her daughter entered the Lansings' home, the maid showed them into the east parlour, where Huybertie saw a whiskerando seated near the fireplace next to Mrs Lansing.

'Why, Herman,' Mrs Pruyn said, 'I didn't expect to see you.'

'Anna,' said the bearded man, warmly greeting her. Mrs Pruyn and Huybertie joined him near the fire.

Abraham Lansing, who had been pouring some madeira when his latest guests arrived, distributed the glasses before proposing a toast.

'To Herman Melville's next book!'

Precisely which book they toasted remains unknown. It had been ten years since *Clarel*, so Lansing's toast may simply reflect wishful thinking. On the other hand, Melville had been assembling his uncollected poems with an eye towards publication. Two years later he would release *John Marr and Other Sailors, with Some Sea-pieces*, with *Timoleon, Etc.* coming out three years after that. Neither can technically be called a publication. Melville issued them in editions of 25 copies each, just enough to distribute to friends and family. No longer would he subject himself to the eyes of the critic or the pocketbooks of the consumer.

In his waning years Melville related to children more easily than adults, a fact Huybertie Pruyn's anecdote reinforces. Eager to engage her in the conversation, Melville asked what she was studying at school.

'Paul Revere's Ride,' she said.

'That is very interesting . . . If you come to my house in New York I will show you a bottle with some tea-leaves in it. The tea came from the Boston Tea Party,' he told her. 'My grandfather, Thomas Melvill, was one of the "Indians" who dumped the tea. He would not tell my grandmother where he had been. But when she cleaned his clothes, she found tea-leaves in the pockets and cuffs. She put the tea in a bottle and kept it.'

There is no further evidence that the vial of tea was then or ever at 26th Street. After Mary Melvill's death it descended to her surviving children, who donated it to the Bostonian Society, where it remains today.[40] Recognizing the unlikelihood of Huybertie coming to Manhattan to visit them, Melville told her a stretcher. Regardless of where the vial was, Melville's words reflect the pride he took in his war-hero grandfather and his desire to perpetuate his memory.

Abraham Lansing's toast was not the only hint Melville received during the 1880s that readers would welcome a new book from his pen. In an 1884 fan letter James Billson told Melville about his circle of like-minded friends in Leicester, England, 'a rapidly increasing knot of "Melville readers"'.[41] Two years later Melville received a similar letter from the British sailor author W. Clark Russell, who became the most vocal Melville enthusiast of the decade, promoting Melville's works in articles and interviews.[42]

Encouraged by the attention, Melville began writing a new novel, the work that would become *Billy Budd*. It started slowly. 'Billy in the Darbies', the poem that ends the novel, Melville wrote first. As he did with some of the poems in *John Marr*, Melville added an explanatory headnote. He could have included the work in *John Marr*, but he expanded the headnote into a short story. Another major stage of revision took *Billy Budd* to book length. Melville never finished the work but brought it close enough to completion for it to achieve recognition as his final masterpiece upon its publication decades later.

'A tale as clear and glowing as a classical medallion', V. S. Pritchett called *Billy Budd*.[43] All the stylistic excess of *Pierre* had disappeared. Like the Burgundy Club sketches, *Billy Budd* possesses an Addisonian clarity that belies the murkiness of its morality. Choosing to prosecute Billy Budd aboard ship for doing no more than acting according to nature, Captain Vere makes him an example to quash the possibility of an incipient mutiny. Billy's execution functions as the blood sacrifice essential for civilization to survive. When Melville went to bed on Sunday, 27 September 1891, he had not quite worked out all the story's details. He never would. Around half past midnight his heart finally gave out.

The year after his death, new editions of *Typee*, *Omoo*, *White-Jacket* and *Moby-Dick* would appear. It's sad that Melville did not live long enough to see these new editions, but the fan letters from England let him know that new readers were discovering his works. The experience of Billson and Russell was repeated elsewhere. Archibald MacMechan encountered a copy of *Moby-Dick* in a Canadian village library and shared his passion for the book with others. In Australia Marcus Clarke read Melville, who became a favourite with Melbourne's community of bohemian writers.[44] Until the Melville revival three decades after his death, little knots of Melville readers around the globe kept the flame alive.

References

Introduction

1 Winifride Wrench, '*Moby Dick* and His Author', *Landmark*, IV (1922), p. 668; W. K. Kelsey, 'Won London in 70 Years', *Kansas City Times*, 2 April 1921, p. 13.

2 Ibid.; H. M. Tomlinson, 'The Phantom Ship', *Observer*, 2 May 1926, p. 7.

3 Wrench, '*Moby Dick*', p. 668; 'Obiter Scripta', *Periodical*, VIII (1921), p. 20; Herbert Read, 'Readers and Writers', *New Age*, 29 September 1921, p. 261; Q. R., *pseud.* [C. Lewis Hind,] 'Herman Melville', *Christian Science Monitor*, 8 November 1921, p. 3.

4 Michael Sadleir, *Excursions in Victorian Bibliography* (London, 1922), p. 217.

5 Leonard Woolf, 'The World of Books: Herman Melville', *Nation and the Athenaeum*, 1 September 1923, p. 688.

6 H. M. Tomlinson, 'A Clue to *Moby Dick*', *Literary Review of the New York Evening Post*, 5 November 1921, p. 1.

7 Quoted in 'Bowling Green', *New York Evening Post*, 5 February 1921, p. 8.

8 Arnold Bennett to André Gide, 2 August 1930, *Correspondance André Gide–Arnold Bennett: Vingt ans d'amitié littéraire (1911–1931)*, ed. Linette F. Brugmans (Paris, 1964), p. 188.

9 [H. W. Massingham,] 'A London Diary', *Nation*, 22 January 1921, p. 572; J. C. Squire, *Books Reviewed* (London, 1922), p. 222.

10 John St Loe Strachey, 'The Complete Works of Herman Melville', *Spectator*, 26 May 1923, p. 887; [Arthur Wallace,] 'Herman Melville's Works', *Manchester Guardian*, 18 April 1923, p. 7; [John Middleton Murry,] 'Herman Melville's Silence', *TLS*, 10 July 1924, p. 433.

11 Woolf, 'World of Books', p. 688; Arnold Bennett, *Arnold Bennett: The Evening Standard Years, 'Books and Persons', 1926–1931* (London, 1974), p. 13.

12 Strachey, 'Complete Works', p. 887.

13 John Freeman, *Herman Melville* (New York, 1926), p. vi.

14 Wrench, '*Moby-Dick*', p. 670.

15 Leland R. Phelps, *Herman Melville's Foreign Reputation: A Research Guide* (Boston, MA, 1983).

16 Kevin J. Hayes and Hershel Parker, *Checklist of Melville Reviews* (Evanston, IL, 1991) (hereafter, *Checklist*), nos. M85, MD139, R90.

17 Maurice Blanchot, 'Le Secret de Melville', *Journal des débats*, 1–2 September 1941, p. 3.

18 Jean-Paul Sartre, '*Moby-Dick* d'Herman Melville: Plus qu'un chef-d'œuvre, un formidable monument', *Comoedia*, 21 June 1941, p. 2.

19 Edward J. Hughes, *Albert Camus* (London, 2015), p. 78.

1 Schools and Schoolmasters

1 'Arrived Since Our Last', *Mercantile Advertiser*, 1 September 1818; 'New French Goods Store', *New-York Daily Advertiser*, 26 October 1818; 'Latest from France', *Mercantile Advertiser*, 8 October 1818; 'New French Goods Store', *Mercantile Advertiser*, 19 September 1818.

2 William H. Gilman, *Melville's Early Life and Redburn* (New York, 1951), p. 14, and Hershel Parker, *Herman Melville: A Biography* (Baltimore, MD, 1996–2002), vol. I, p. 11, say Allan opened the business in November.

3 S.V.S. Wilder, *Records from the Life of S.V.S. Wilder* (New York, 1865), pp. 45–7.

4 'The Tea Party', *Boston Evening Transcript*, 15 December 1873, p. 6.

5 Merton M. Sealts Jr, *Melville's Reading*, revd edn (Columbia, NY, 1988), no. 142.

6 William P. Blake and Lemuel Blake, *Catalogue of Books, for Sale or Circulation . . . at the Boston Book-store* (Boston, MA, 1798); Sealts, *Melville's Reading*, no. 69.

7 *The Athenaeum Centenary: The Influence and History of the Boston Athenaeum* (Boston, MA, 1907), p. 127.

8 Sealts, *Melville's Reading*, no. 103.

9 'For Sale or To Let', *New-York Evening Post*, 16 September 1818.

10 'Valuable Real Estate', *New-York Evening Post*, 26 December 1823.

11 Jay Leyda, *The Melville Log* (New York, 1969), vol. I, p. 19.

12 Harrison Hayford, G. Thomas Tanselle and Hershel Parker, eds, *The Writings of Herman Melville* (Evanston, IL, 1968–) (hereafter, *Writings*), vol. VIII, p. 150.

13 Ibid., p. 61.

14 Leyda, *Melville Log*, vol. I, p. 20.

15 Parker, *Herman Melville*, vol. I, p. 302; *Macbeth*, IV.i.14–15.

16 John Griscom, *Monitorial Instruction: An Address, Pronounced at the Opening of the New-York High-School* (New York, 1825), pp. 44–6; Parker, *Herman Melville*, vol. I, p. 95.

17 'Griscom's Long Fast', *New York Sun*, 19 June 1881, p. 5.

18 Cornelius Mathews, *Big Abel, and the Little Manhattan* (New York, 1845), p. v.

19 [Anne Newport Royall,] *Sketches of History, Life, and Manners in the United States* (New Haven, CT, 1826), p. 257.

20 Austin Baldwin, *A Table Book, and Primary Arithmetic, Compiled and Arranged for the Introductory Department of the New York High Schools* (1829; New York, 1843), p. 6.

21 Ibid., pp. 6, 26.

22 Ibid., p. 40.

23 'New York High Schools', *New-York Evening Post*, 19 May 1829.

24 'View of the New-York High School', *Cabinet of Instruction, Literature, and Amusement*, I (1829), pp. 625–6; Leyda, *Melville Log*, vol. I, p. 32; 'Boarding and Day School', *New-York Evening Post*, 8 May 1827.

25 '440 Broome-Street', *New-York Evening Post*, 15 September 1827; Leyda, *Melville Log*, vol. I, p. 32; *Writings*, vol. IV, p. 79.

26 *Writings*, vol. IV, p. 122; *The American First Class Book; or, Exercises in Reading and Recitation*, ed. John Pierpont (Boston, MA, 1823), pp. 286–7.

27 *The Literary and Scientific Class Book*, ed. Levi L. Leonard (Keene, NH, 1827), pp. 281–2.

28 *First Annual Report of the American Tract Society, Instituted at New-York, 1825* (New York, 1826), p. 47; *Writings*, vol. IV, p. 139.

29 *Second Annual Report of the American Tract Society* (New York, 1827), p. 60.

30 Gansevoort Melvill to Maria Melvill, 23 May 1829 [misdated 1828], in John P. Runden, 'Columbia Grammar School: An Overlooked Year in the Lives of Gansevoort and Herman Melville', *Melville Society Extracts*, no. 46 (1981), p. 2.

31 *Writings*, vol. IV, pp. 80, 172.
32 John P. Runden, 'Old School Ties: Melville, the Columbia Grammar School, and the New Yorkers', *Melville Society Extracts*, no. 55 (1983), p. 4; Leyda, *Melville Log*, vol. I, p. 49.
33 Runden, 'Old School Ties', pp. 1–5.
34 Runden, 'Columbia Grammar School', p. 2; Robert Tomes, *My College Days* (New York, 1880), p. 20.
35 Tomes, *My College Days*, pp. 20–21.
36 *Writings*, vol. VIII, p. 144.
37 Tomes, *My College Days*, pp. 9–10.
38 William Shakespeare, *Comedies, Histories, Tragedies, and Poems*, ed. Richard Grant White (Boston, MA, 1883), vol. II, p. 773.
39 Sealts, *Melville's Reading*, no. 103.
40 Parker, *Herman Melville*, vol. I, p. 49.
41 Leyda, *Melville Log*, vol. I, p. 45.
42 Ibid.
43 Parker, *Herman Melville*, vol. I, p. 51.
44 David K. Titus, 'Herman Melville at the Albany Academy', *Melville Society Extracts*, no. 42 (1980), pp. 1, 4–10.
45 Gilman, *Melville's Early Life*, p. 54.
46 'Albany Academy', *Albany Argus*, 6 August 1831.
47 Jesse Olney, *A Practical System of Modern Geography* (Hartford, CT, 1829), p. 42.
48 'Meeting of Chicago Principals', *Public-school Journal*, XII (1893), p. 429.
49 Kevin J. Hayes, *Melville's Folk Roots* (Kent, OH, 1999), p. 85.
50 Leyda, *Melville Log*, vol. I, 48; Sealts, *Melville's Reading*, no. 331.
51 Titus, 'Herman Melville at the Albany Academy', p. 7.
52 Parker, *Herman Melville*, vol. I, p. 56, mentions without identifying Joseph Greenleaf, whose name appears in numerous advertisements for money to lend. See, for example, *New York Daily Advertiser*, 16 May 1831.
53 Parker, *Herman Melville*, vol. I, p. 56.
54 Leyda, *Melville Log*, vol. I, p. 50.
55 Ibid., p. 51.
56 Parker, *Herman Melville*, vol. I, p. 427.
57 *Writings*, vol. IV, p. 36.

2 Work

1 Cuyler Reynolds, *Albany Chronicles: A History of the City Arranged Chronologically* (Albany, NY, 1906), p. 491.

2 Jay Leyda, *The Melville Log* (New York, 1969), vol. I, p. 56.

3 Jay Leyda, 'An Albany Journal by Gansevoort Melville', *Boston Public Library Quarterly*, II (1950), pp. 337, 345.

4 *Writings*, vol. IX, p. 41.

5 *Writings*, vol. VI, p. 194.

6 Hershel Parker, *Herman Melville: A Biography* (Baltimore, MD, 1996–2002), vol. I, p. 114.

7 Ibid., p. 115.

8 *Annual Report of the Regents of the University of the State of New-York* (Albany, NY, 1836), p. 58.

9 *Writings*, vol. IX, p. 191.

10 'To Clear To-day and Sail To-morrow', *Liverpool Mercury*, 2 August 1839.

11 *Writings*, vol. IV, pp. 166–7.

12 'A Canny Craft and Her Captain', *Belfast News-letter*, 30 October 1849 (not in *Checklist*).

13 *Writings*, vol. VI, p. 249.

14 *Writings*, vol. IV, p. 221.

15 *Writings*, vol. III, p. 291.

16 Calvin Colton, *Tour of the American Lakes, and among the Indians of the North-west Territory, in 1830* (London, 1833), vol. I, p. 37.

17 Ibid., p. 58.

18 *Writings*, vol. VI, p. 244; vol. III, p. 615.

19 Richard Gear Hobbs, 'Autobiography of Clarissa Emely Gear Hobbs', *Journal of the Illinois State Historical Society*, XVII (1925), pp. 633–4.

20 Kevin J. Hayes, *The Cambridge Introduction to Herman Melville* (Cambridge, 2007), p. 3.

21 HM to Richard Henry Dana, 1 May 1850, *Writings*, vol. XIV, p. 160.

22 *Writings*, vol. IX, p. 205.

23 Ibid., p. 207. The quotation in the following paragraph comes from J. Ross Browne, *Etchings of a Whaling Cruise* (New York, 1846), p. 11.

24 *Writings*, vol. XIV, p. 24.

25 Hershel Parker, *Melville Biography: An Inside Narrative* (Evanston, IL,

2012), p. 135; Richard T. Greene to the Editor of the *Buffalo Commercial Advertiser*, 1 July 1845, *Writings*, vol. XIV, p. 579.

26 Richard Henry Dana Jr, *Two Years Before the Mast* (New York, 1840), p. 9.

27 Quoted in Minna Littman, 'Edgartown Finds New Link with Melville', New Bedford *Sunday Standard*, 11 August 1929, section IV, p. 31.

28 *Writings*, vol. IX, p. 210.

29 Browne, *Etchings*, pp. 35–7.

30 Wilson Heflin, *Herman Melville's Whaling Years*, ed. Mary K. Bercaw Edwards and Thomas Farel Heffernan (Nashville, TN, 2004), p. 59.

31 *Writings*, vol. IX, pp. 209–10.

32 *Writings*, vol. V, p. 96.

33 *Writings*, vol. VI, p. 983.

34 Heflin, *Herman Melville's Whaling Years*, pp. 26–8.

35 Kevin J. Hayes, 'Toby's *Typee* Lecture', *Melville Society Extracts*, no. 96 (1994), pp. 1–4; Richard T. Greene to HM, 8 April 1861, *Writings*, vol. XIV, p. 686.

36 Heflin, *Herman Melville's Whaling Years*, p. 81.

37 *Writings*, vol. I, p. 15.

38 Robert Buchanan, *The Outcast: A Rhyme for the Time* (London, 1891), p. 77.

39 In his annotated copy of John Todd, *Index Rerum: or, Index of Subjects* (Northampton, MA, 1837) at the Berkshire Athenaeum, Gansevoort Melville recorded reading 'Storm in the Southern Ocean', *New World*, 4 June 1842, p. 356.

40 Quoted in Philip Young, *The Private Melville* (University Park, PA, 1993), p. 41.

41 Richard T. Greene to the Editor of the *Buffalo Commercial Advertiser*, 1 July 1845, *Writings*, vol. XIV, p. 581.

42 Heflin, *Herman Melville's Whaling Years*, p. 161; Parker, *Herman Melville*, vol. I, p. 219.

43 'Revolt Documents', *Omoo: A Narrative of Adventures in the South Seas*, ed. Harrison Hayford and Walter Blair (New York, 1969), pp. 338–9.

44 William G. Libbey, 'Quondam Sailor', *Shaker Manifesto*, VIII (1878), p. 280.

45 'Improvements and Changes in and about Honolulu', *Polynesian*, 17 October 1840, p. 74.

46 *Writings*, vol. III, p. 273.

47 Robert S. Forsythe, 'Herman Melville in Honolulu', *New England*

Quarterly, VIII (1935), p. 101; Heflin, *Herman Melville's Whaling Years*, p. 190.

48 Robert Tomes, 'A Night and Day at Valparaiso', in *Gifts of Genius: A Miscellany of Prose and Poetry* (New York, 1859), pp. 173–4.

49 *Writings*, vol. III, p. 104.

50 *Writings*, vol. II, p. 228.

51 *Writings*, vol. VI, p. 193.

3 The New Robinson Crusoe

1 [Nathaniel P. Willis,] 'Literary Notices', *Home Journal*, 24 November 1849 (*Checklist*, no. R56); Merton M. Sealts, *The Early Lives of Melville: Nineteenth-century Biographical Sketches and their Authors* (Madison, WI, 1974), p. 128, the source of the following quotation.

2 *Writings*, vol. I, p. 109.

3 Ibid., p. 244.

4 [Richard Grant White,] *Law and Laziness; or, Students at Law of Leisure* (New York, 1846), p. 6.

5 Edwin Fussell, *Frontier: American Literature and the American West* (Princeton, NJ, 1965), p. 313; *Gansevoort Melville's 1846 London Journal and Letters from England, 1845*, ed. Hershel Parker (New York, 1966), p. 33.

6 Victor Hugo Paltsits, 'Herman Melville's Background and New Light on the Publication of *Typee*', *Bookmen's Holiday: Notes and Studies Written and Gathered in Tribute to Harry Miller Lydenberg* (New York, 1943), p. 256.

7 Paltsits, 'Herman Melville's Background', p. 256.

8 Hershel Parker, *Melville Biography: An Inside Narrative* (Evanston, IL, 2012), pp. 149–52.

9 Angus Fraser, 'John Murray's Colonial and Home Library', *PBSA*, XCI (1997), pp. 339–41, 371.

10 George Paston, *pseud.* [Emily Morse Symonds,] 'From the Archives of Albemarle Street: I. In the Forties', *Cornhill Magazine*, LXIX (1930), p. 137.

11 Angus Fraser, 'A Publishing House and Its Readers, 1841–1880: The Murrays and the Miltons', *PBSA*, XC (1996), p. 29.

12 *Gansevoort Melville's 1846 London Journal*, pp. 20–22.

13 'Literature', *Magnet*, 2 March 1846; 'Literature', *Hampshire Advertiser and Salisbury Guardian*, 14 March 1846 (neither in *Checklist*).

14 'The Literary Era', *Era*, 19 April 1846 (not in *Checklist*).

15 Brian Higgins and Hershel Parker, eds, *Herman Melville: The Contemporary Reviews* (Cambridge, 1995) (hereafter, *Contemporary Reviews*), p. 28. 'The New Robinson Crusoe', *New York Herald*, 28 April 1846; 'Typee, or A Residence in the Marquesas Islands', *Richmond Inquirer*, 30 June 1846 (neither in *Checklist*).

16 *Writings*, vol. VI, p. 5.

17 Daniel Defoe, *The Life and Adventures of Robinson Crusoe* (London, 1937), pp. 18–19.

18 HM to Gansevoort Melville, 29 May 1846, *Writings*, vol. XIV, p. 41.

19 H. C., 'Typee: A Peep at Polynesian Life', *New-York Evangelist*, 9 April 1846 (*Checklist*, no. T65).

20 HM to Evert A. Duyckinck, 15(?) July 1846, *Writings*, vol. XIV, p. 53.

21 'All Sorts of Paragraphs', *Boston Post*, 29 June 1846; Hershel Parker, *Herman Melville: A Biography* (Baltimore, MD, 1996–2002), vol. I, pp. 426–7.

22 *Writings*, vol. II, p. 149.

23 Ibid., p. 102.

24 Fraser, 'Publishing House', p. 29.

25 *Writings*, vol. II, p. 241.

26 HM to John Murray, 29 January 1847, *Writings*, vol. XIV, p. 78.

27 Ibid.

28 HM, *The Works of Herman Melville*, ed. Michael Sadleir (London, 1922–4), vol. XIII, p. 362; *Writings*, vol. XIV, p. 541.

29 Robert Tomes, *Battles of America by Sea and Land with Biographies of Naval and Military Commanders* (New York, 1861), vol. II, p. 517.

30 *Writings*, vol. XI, p. 203.

31 HM, *Works*, vol. XIII, p. 361.

32 K. Jack Bauer, *Surfboats and Horse Marines: U.S. Naval Operations in the Mexican War, 1846–48* (Annapolis, MD, 1969), pp. 81–2; 'Extracts from the Correspondence of the N.O. [New Orleans] Tropic', *New York Evening Express*, 3 April 1847.

33 Tomes, *Battles of America*, vol. II, p. 517.

34 Amelia E. Barr, *All the Days of My Life: An Autobiography* (New York, 1913), pp. 390–91.

35 Paltsits, 'Herman Melville's Background', pp. 256–7, prints Saunders's account from a manuscript at the New York Public Library.

36 'Fun at Sea', *Lowell Daily Courier*, 6 July 1847; 'Fun at Sea', *Huntington Long-Islander*, 17 December 1847 (neither in *Checklist*).

37 [Frederick Hardman,] 'Pacific Rovings', *Blackwood's Edinburgh Magazine*, LXI (1847), pp. 755, 757 (*Checklist*, no. 080 [unattributed]).

38 'From Adventures in the South Seas', *New Zealander*, 27 October 1849 (not in *Checklist*).

39 'A Maori Harpooneer', *New Zealand Spectator*, 6 November 1847; 'A Maori Harpooneer', *New Zealander*, 2 February 1848; 'A Maori Harpooner', *Colonial Intelligencer*, II (1849–50), 95 (none in *Checklist*).

40 *Contemporary Reviews*, p. 143.

41 Charles Fenno Hoffman, 'From an Unsigned Review', in *Melville: The Critical Heritage*, ed. Watson G. Branch (London, 1974), p. 98.

42 [Caroline M. Kirkland,] 'Editorial Miscellany', *Union Magazine of Literature and Art*, I (1847), p. 96 (not in *Checklist*).

43 Parker, *Herman Melville*, vol. I, p. 410; Sealts, *Early Lives*, p. 174.

44 Parker, *Herman Melville*, vol. I, p. 541.

45 Jay Leyda, *The Melville Log* (New York, 1969), vol. I, pp. 249, 254, 293.

46 HM, *Works*, vol. XVI, p. 303.

4 The Fight of All Fights

1 Grace Gayfeather, *pseud*., 'Leaves by the Way-side', *New England Offering*, January 1850, p. 10; HM to Lemuel Shaw, 6 August 1847, *Writings*, vol. XIV, p. 96.

2 *Writings*, vol. VI, pp. 4, 193; vol. XV, p. 18.

3 Jay Leyda, *The Melville Log* (New York, 1969), vol. I, p. 257; *Writings*, vol. V, p. 75.

4 Elizabeth Melville to Hope Shaw, 21 August 1847, in Eleanor Melville Metcalf, *Herman Melville: Cycle and Epicycle* (Cambridge, MA, 1953), p. 45; *Writings*, vol. III, p. 492.

5 Leyda, *Melville Log*, vol. I, p. 257.

6 Hershel Parker, *Herman Melville: A Biography* (Baltimore, MD, 1996–2002), vol. I, p. 548.

7 *Writings*, vol. III, p. 376.

8 Parker, *Herman Melville*, vol. I, p. 553; 'To Let – From the 1st', *New York Herald*, 22 March 1866, p. 7; Leyda, *Melville Log*, vol. I, p. 264.

9 Edgar Allan Poe, *Essays and Reviews*, ed. G. R. Thompson (New York, 1984), p. 1136.

10 Quoted in 'Our Portrait', *Knickerbocker*, LII (1858), p. 173.

11 Merton M. Sealts Jr, *Melville's Reading*, revd edn (Columbia, SC, 1988) nos. 102–3.

12 *Writings*, vol. III, p. 5.

13 Ibid., p. 229.

14 Nathalia Wright, 'Melville and "Old Burton", with "Bartleby" as an Anatomy of Melancholy', *Tennessee Studies in Literature*, XV (1970), p. 2.

15 *Writings*, vol. III, p. 229.

16 Ibid.

17 Ibid., p. 230.

18 Ibid.

19 'The Melvilles', *North American*, 7 May 1850.

20 *Transactions of the American Art Union, for the Year 1847* (New York, 1848), p. 75.

21 'The American Art Union', *New York Evening Mirror*, 7 October 1847; Leyda, *Melville Log*, vol. I, p. 262.

22 *Writings*, vol. III, p. 297.

23 Leyda, *Melville Log*, vol. I, p. 266.

24 Leonard Woolf, 'The World of Books: Herman Melville', *Nation and the Athenaeum*, 1 September 1923, p. 688.

25 *Writings*, vol. III, pp. 352, 172 (my emphasis); Brian Foley, 'Herman Melville and the Example of Sir Thomas Browne', in *The Critical Response to Herman Melville's Moby-Dick*, ed. Kevin J. Hayes (Westport, CT, 1994), pp. 205–6.

26 *Writings*, vol. III, p. 228.

27 Leyda, *Melville Log*, vol. I, p. 273; Howard A. Kelly and Walter L. Burrage, *American Medical Biographies* (Baltimore, MD, 1920), p. 1152.

28 *Commemoration on Board U.S. Mail Steamer Hermann, Lieut. Edward Higgins, U.S.N., Commander, on Her Passage from Bremen to New York, July Fourth, 1853* (New York, 1853).

29 HM to John Murray, 25 March 1848, *Writings*, vol. XIV, pp. 106–7.

30 HM to John Murray, 19 June 1848, *Writings*, vol. XIV, p. 109.

31 Leyda, *Melville Log*, vol. I, p. 276; Leonard Woolf, 'World of Books', p. 688.

32 Leyda, *Melville Log*, vol. I, p. 277.

33 Ibid., p. 278.

34 Jorge Luis Borges, *Selected Non-fictions*, trans. Esther Allen, Suzanne Jill Levine and Eliot Weinberger (New York, 1999), p. 246.

35 *Writings*, vol. III, p. 594.

36 Ibid., p. 595.

37 Sealts, *Melville's Reading*, no. 174; Lea Bertani Vozar Newman, 'Melville's Copy of Dante: Evidence of New Connections between the *Commedia* and *Mardi*', *Studies in the American Renaissance*, ed. Joel Myerson (Charlottesville, VA, 1993), pp. 305–38.

38 *Writings*, vol. III, p. 654.

39 Albert Camus, *Lyrical and Critical Essays*, ed. Philip Thody, trans. Ellen Conroy Kennedy (New York, 1970), p. 291.

40 Angus Fraser, 'A Publishing House and Its Readers, 1841–1880: The Murray and the Miltons', *PBSA*, XC (1996), p. 31.

41 Lynn Horth, 'Richard Bentley's Place in Melville's Literary Career', in *Studies in the American Renaissance*, ed. Myerson, p. 231.

42 'Herman Melville', *Standard*, 10 April 1849 (not in *Checklist*).

43 'A Page by the Author of *Mardi*', *Man in the Moon*, V (1849), pp. 284–5 (*Checklist*, no. M71).

44 'Our Table', *Montreal Literary Garland*, VII (1849), p. 192 (not in *Checklist*).

45 *Contemporary Reviews*, p. 225.

5 London

1 *Writings*, vol. XV, p. 12. Details of HM's trip come from his journal, pp. 3–48, and will not be cited separately.

2 *Writings*, vol. VI, p. 69.

3 HM to the Editor of the *Albany Microscope*, 31 March 1838, *Writings*, vol. XIV, p. 19, traces debating societies to Franklin's junto, indicating HM's familiarity with Franklin's *Autobiography*.

4 [George Ripley,] 'Reviews of New Books', *New-York Daily Tribune*, 10 May 1849 (*Checklist*, no. M80).

5   See Nigel Cliff, *The Shakespeare Riots: Revenge, Drama, and Death in Nineteenth-century America* (New York, 2007).

6   James Fenimore Cooper to Susan Cooper, 10 May 1849, *Letters and Journals*, ed. James Franklin Beard (Cambridge, MA, 1960–68), vol. VI, p. 39.

7   A. Oakey Hall, 'Riots in New York', *New York Press*, 31 August 1890, p. 4.

8   [J. St Loe Strachey,] 'Herman Melville', *Spectator*, 24 June 1893, p. 859.

9   John Seelye, *Melville: The Ironic Diagram* (Evanston, IL, 1970), p. 32.

10   HM to Richard Bentley, 5 June 1849, *Writings*, vol. XIV, p. 132.

11   *The Exchequer Reports: Reports of Cases Argued and Determined in the Courts of Exchequer and Exchequer Chamber*, vol. IV: *Trinity Term, 12 Vict. to Hilary Term, 13 Vict.*, ed. W. N. Welsby, E. T. Hurlstone and J. Gordon (London, 1851), p. 145.

12   Richard Bentley to HM, 20 June 1849, *Writings*, vol. XIV, p. 596.

13   *Contemporary Reviews*, p. 319.

14   Kevin J. Hayes, *The Cambridge Introduction to Herman Melville* (Cambridge, 2007), p. 21.

15   *Writings*, vol. V, p. 322.

16   V. S. Pritchett, 'Without the Whale', *New Statesman*, 19 April 1958, p. 504.

17   *Writings*, vol. XV, p. 13.

18   'Redburn', *Morning Chronicle*, 28 November 1849 (not in *Checklist*).

19   [Joseph Milsand,] 'Bulletin Bibliographique', *Revue des deux mondes*, V (1850), pp. 380–82 (*Checklist*, no. R90 [unattributed]).

20   'The American Bowling Saloon', *Atlas*, 2 June 1849, p. 348.

21   *Writings*, vol. V, p. 94

22   *Writings*, vol. XV, p. 14.

23   *Writings*, vol. VIII, p. 159.

24   *Writings*, vol. VI, p. 470.

25   Ibid., p. 155.

26   'Valuable Books at Very Low Prices', *Athenaeum*, 27 January 1849, p. 82; 'The Late Mr E. W. Stibbs', *Publishers' Circular*, 9 May 1891, p. 472; 'Choice Second Hand Books', *Literary World*, 11 August 1849, p. 120; Merton M. Sealts Jr, *Melville's Reading*, revd edn (Columbia, SC, 1988), nos. 53, 302.

27   Clement Scott and Cecil Howard, *The Life and Reminiscences of E. L. Blanchard* (London, 1891), vol. II, p. 427; George C. Boase, 'Edward

Leman Blanchard and the "Edinburgh Castle" Tavern', *Notes and Queries*, 7th ser., XII (1891), pp. 402–3; *Writings*, vol. XV, pp. 18–19.

28 *Writings*, vol. XV, pp. 19, 4; Lyman R. Bradley, 'George J. Adler, 1821–1868', *German Quarterly*, VII (1934), p. 154; 'Mail Gleanings', *Philadelphia Inquirer*, 28 August 1868, p. 8.

29 'C. F. Hoffman', *New-York Tribune*, 21 April 1849; 'Charles F. Hoffman', *Literary Union*, 5 May 1849, p. 75.

30 HM to Evert A. Duyckinck, 5 April 1849, *Writings*, vol. XIV, p. 128.

31 Hayes, *Cambridge Introduction*, p. 101.

32 *Writings*, vol. VI, p. 39.

33 'Literature', *Caledonian Mercury*, 11 March 1850 (not in *Checklist*).

34 'Midshipmen Entering the Navy Early', *Southern Press*, 23 October 1850 (not in *Checklist*).

35 Caroline M. Kirkland to Unknown, 26 March 1850, *The Letters of Caroline M. Kirkland*, ed. Audrey J. Roberts (Ann Arbor, MI, 1976), p. 263; *Writings*, vol. XV, p. 6.

36 'Flogging in the Navy', *Boston Investigator*, 17 April 1850; 'Flogging in the Navy', Gettysburg *Star and Banner*, 19 April 1850 (neither in *Checklist*).

37 *Writings*, vol. V, p. 146; 'Flogging in the Navy', *Brooklyn Daily Eagle*, 10 April 1850.

38 'The United States', *Morning Chronicle*, 11 October 1850 (not in *Checklist*).

39 *Writings*, vol. XV, pp. 44, 47; W. K. Kelsey, 'Won London in 70 Years', *Kansas City Times*, 2 April 1921, p. 13.

6 Wild Impetuous Grandeur

1 Mary Gove Nichols to Alonzo Lewis, 13 March [1850], Clifton Waller Barrett Library, accession no. 14020, Special Collections, University of Virginia Library, Charlottesville, VA.

2 HM to Evert Duyckinck, 2 February 1850, *Writings*, vol. XIV, p. 154.

3 HM to Richard Henry Dana Jr, 1 May 1850, *Writings*, vol. XIV, p. 162.

4 Merton M. Sealts Jr, *Melville's Reading*, revd edn (Columbia, SC, 1988), nos. 52, 450–51.

5 HM to Richard Bentley, 27 June 1850, *Writings*, vol. XIV, p. 163.

6 Jay Leyda, *The Melville Log* (New York, 1969), vol. I, p. 378;
   'The Melvilles', *North American and United States Gazette*, 7 May 1850;
   'The Melvilles', *Tarborough Press*, 7 September 1850.

7 'Berkshire Social Events, August 1850', in *Melville in His Own Time*,
   ed. Steven Olsen-Smith (Iowa City, IA, 2015), pp. 35, 43.

8 Ibid., pp. 36, 52.

9 Ibid., pp. 38–9.

10 *Writings*, vol. VI, p. 314.

11 Kevin J. Hayes, *Melville's Folk Roots* (Kent, OH, 1999), pp. 3–4.

12 Hershel Parker, *Herman Melville: A Biography* (Baltimore, MD,
   1996–2002), vol. I, pp. 755–6.

13 HM to Evert A. Duyckinck, 16 August 1850, *Writings*, vol. XIV, p. 167.

14 Parker, *Herman Melville*, vol. I, p. 779.

15 'Library for Pittsfield', *Massachusetts Eagle*, 4 January 1850; Pittsfield
   Library Association, *Annual Report, Constitution and By-laws, Catalogue
   &c.* (Pittsfield, PA, 1852).

16 *Writings*, vol. VII, p. 283.

17 Thomas Beale, *The Natural History of the Sperm Whale* (London, 1839),
   p. iii (HM copy, Houghton Library, Harvard University).

18 Leyda, *Melville Log*, vol. I, p. 396.

19 Parker, *Herman Melville*, vol. I, p. 792.

20 Hayes, *Melville's Folk Roots*, p. 87.

21 Caroline Gilman, *Oracles from the Poets: A Fanciful Diversion for the
   Drawing-room* (New York, 1844), p. 207.

22 Ibid., pp. 28, 27.

23 HM to Evert Duyckinck, 13 December 1850, *Writings*, vol. XIV, p. 174.

24 *Writings*, vol. VI, p. 370.

25 Jean-Paul Sartre, '*Moby-Dick* d'Herman Melville: Plus qu'un chef-
   d'œuvre, un formidable monument', *Comoedia*, 21 June 1941, p. 2.

26 Robert Sattelmeyer, '"Shanties of Chapters and Essays": Rewriting
   Moby-Dick', *ESQ*, XLIX (2003), pp. 213–47; Harrison Hayford,
   'Unnecessary Duplicates: A Key to the Writing of *Moby-Dick*', in *New
   Perspectives on Melville*, ed. Faith Pullin (Edinburgh, 1978), pp. 128–61.

27 Maurice Blanchot, 'Le Secret de Melville', *Journal des débats* (1–2
   September 1941), p. 3.

28 Parker, *Herman Melville*, vol. I, p. 810.

29 HM to Nathaniel Hawthorne, [29 January?] 1851, *Writings*, vol. XIV, p. 176.

30 Leyda, *Melville Log*, vol. I, p. 407.

31 Nathaniel Hawthorne, *Tales and Sketches*, ed. Roy Harvey Pearce (New York, 1982), p. 1301.

32 Parker, *Herman Melville*, vol. I, p. 821; HM to Nathaniel Hawthorne, 29 June 1851, *Writings*, vol. XIV, p. 195.

33 *Writings*, vol. VI, p. 55.

34 Ibid., p. 107.

35 *Writings*, vol. VI, p. 62.

36 Here I follow Sattelmeyer, 'Shanties of Chapters', p. 238, who places the two sections at the same stage of composition. Alternatively, Hershel Parker, '*Moby-Dick* and Domesticity', in *Critical Essays on Herman Melville's Moby-Dick*, ed. Brian Higgins and Hershel Parker (New York, 1992), p. 557, dates them months apart.

37 *Writings*, vol. VI, p. 416.

38 Jorge Luis Borges, *Selected Non-fictions*, trans. Esther Allen, Suzanne Jill Levine and Eliot Weinberger (New York, 1999), p. 245.

39 Kevin J. Hayes, *The Cambridge Introduction to Herman Melville* (Cambridge, 2007), pp. 46–7.

40 James Geddes Craighead, *The Craighead Family: A Genealogical Memoir of the Descendants of Rev. Thomas and Margaret Craighead, 1658–1876* (Philadelphia, PA, 1876), p. 133.

41 *Writings*, vol. VII, p. 338.

42 Ibid., p. 340.

43 *Writings*, vol. VI, p. 434 (my emphasis).

44 Parker, *Herman Melville*, vol. I, p. 863.

45 *Writings*, vol. VI, p. 52.

46 [Edward Forbes,] 'The Whale', *Literary Gazette*, 6 December 1851, p. 841 (*Checklist*, no. MD101 [unattributed]); Edward Forbes, *Literary Papers* (London, 1855), p. 159.

47 *Writings*, vol. VI, pp. 142–3.

48 Forbes, *Literary Papers*, p. 159.

49 [Angus Bethune Reach,] 'Town Talk and Table Talk', *Illustrated London News*, 1 November 1851, p. 539 (*Checklist*, no. MD18 [unattributed]).

50 [George Henry Lewes,] 'Herman Melville', London *Leader*, 8 November 1851, p. 1068 (*Checklist*, no. MD25 [unattributed]).

51 'Literature', *Daily News*, 12 January 1852 (not in *Checklist*).

52 'The Whale', *Morning Post*, 20 October 1851 (not in *Checklist*).
53 'Editors' Table', *Independent*, 20 November 1851, p. 192 (*Checklist*, no. MD60).
54 [Evert Duyckinck,] 'Melville's *Moby-Dick; or, The Whale*: Second Notice', *Literary World*, 22 November 1851, p. 403 (*Checklist*, no. MD69).
55 *Writings*, vol. VI, p. xviii.
56 [Duyckinck,] 'Melville's *Moby-Dick*', p. 404.

7 The Calamities of Authorship

1 V. S. Pritchett, 'Without the Whale', *New Statesman*, 19 April 1958, p. 504.
2 *Writings*, vol. VII, p. 51.
3 *Writings*, vol. VI, p. 44.
4 *Writings*, vol. VII, p. 66.
5 Quoted in Hershel Parker, *Herman Melville: A Biography* (Baltimore, MD, 1996–2002), vol. II, p. 47.
6 Hershel Parker, 'Introduction', in *Pierre: or, The Ambiguities* (New York, 1995), p. xxxii.
7 Ibid., pp. xxxiii–xxxv.
8 Ibid., pp. xxxv–xxxix.
9 *Contemporary Reviews*, p. 433.
10 Quoted in [Elizabeth Oakes Smith,] 'The Seven Travellers', *Emerson's Magazine*, VII (1858), p. 462.
11 William Gilmore Simms, *Selected Reviews on Literature and Civilization*, ed. James Evert Kibler Jr and David Moltke-Hansen (Columbia, SC, 2014), p. 122.
12 'History of the Last Illness of Goethe', *Medico-chirurgical Review*, XX (1834), p. 499.
13 [Fitz-James O'Brien,] 'Our Young Authors – Melville', *Putnam's Monthly*, I (1853), p. 164 (*Checklist*, no. G22).
14 Quoted in Hershel Parker, 'Herman Melville's *The Isle of the Cross*: A Survey and a Chronology', *American Literature*, LXII (1990), p. 12.
15 Parker, 'Herman Melville's *The Isle of the Cross*', p. 16.
16 'Putnam's Monthly', Syracuse *Evening Chronicle*, 21 November 1853 (not in *Checklist*).
17 Edwin Muir, 'Herman Melville', *Observer*, 4 March 1951, p. 7.

18 *Writings*, vol. IX, p. 1.

19 Ibid., p. 12.

20 Muir, 'Herman Melville', p. 7.

21 Milwaukee *Daily Free Democrat*, 5 June 1856 (not in *Checklist*).

22 New York *Evening Express*, 20 June 1856 (not in *Checklist*).

23 Jay Leyda, *The Melville Log* (New York, 1969), vol. II, p. 523.

24 Leyda, *Melville Log*, vol. II, pp. 930, 524; Merton M. Sealts Jr, *Melville's Reading*, revd edn (Columbia, SC, 1988), no. 528.

25 William Andrews, *Bygone Cheshire* (Chester, 1895), p. 96.

26 *Writings*, vol. XV, p. 80.

27 Ibid., p. 81.

28 Ibid., pp. 93–4.

29 Ibid., p. 101.

30 Bruce Chatwin, 'Pompeii: Same Old Humanity', *Spectator*, 4 December 1976, p. 30.

31 Parker, *Herman Melville*, vol. II, p. 467.

8 The Modern Ossian

1 *Writings*, vol. XI, p. 893.

2 Stanton Garner, *The Civil War World of Herman Melville* (Lawrence, KS, 1993), p. 310.

3 Ibid., p. 315.

4 Jonathan A. Cook, 'History, Legend, and Poetic Tradition in Melville's "The Scout toward Aldie"', *ATQ*, XVII (2003), p. 63.

5 Ibid.

6 *Writings*, vol. XI, p. 140.

7 *Writings*, vol. IX, p. 411; Walker Cowen, *Melville's Marginalia* (New York, 1987), vol. II, p. 193.

8 *Writings*, vol. XI, p. 73.

9 'New Books', *Indianapolis Daily Journal*, 15 December 1866, p. 7 (not in *Checklist*).

10 *Contemporary Reviews*, p. 545.

11 Samuel Arthur Jones, 'Epistolary Remarks, 1900', in *Melville in His Own Time*, ed. Steven Olsen-Smith (Iowa City, IA, 2015), p. 127.

12 Oscar Wegelin, 'Herman Melville as I Remember Him', in *Melville in His Own Time*, ed. Olsen-Smith, p. 150.

13 Jay Leyda, *The Melville Log* (New York, 1969), vol. II, p. 688.

14 Ibid., p. 690.

15 HM to Maria Melville, 5 May 1870, *Writings*, vol. XIV, p. 412.

16 Ibid.

17 'The Boston Tea Party', *New-York Daily Tribune*, 17 December 1873, p. 4.

18 John Freeman, *Herman Melville* (London, 1926), p. 166.

19 Walker Percy, 'Herman Melville', *New Criterion*, 1 November 1983, p. 41.

20 See, for example, William Potter, *Melville's Clarel and the Intersympathy of Creeds* (Kent, OH, 2004).

21 *Writings*, vol. XII, p. 486.

22 Leyda, *Melville Log*, vol. II, p. 748.

23 *The White Mountains: A Handbook for Travellers*, 4th edn (Boston, MA, 1881), p. 182.

24 Quoted in Eleanor Melville Metcalf, *Herman Melville: Cycle and Epicycle* (Cambridge, MA, 1953), p. 251.

25 France Thomas Osborne, 'Childhood Recollections, 1965', in *Melville in His Own Time*, ed. Olsen-Smith, p. 157.

26 Metcalf, *Herman Melville*, p. 259.

27 Quoted in Minna Littman, 'Edgartown Finds New Link with Melville', New Bedford *Sunday Standard*, 11 August 1929, section IV, p. 31.

28 Ibid.

29 'New-Jersey Battles Celebrated', *New York Times*, 4 January 1894, p. 9.

30 Thomas, like most serious cyclists of the era, preferred a high wheeler over a safety bicycle. Thomas's friend L. H. Porter said Essex County roads were so good that 'a safety machine is a superfluity, if not an absurdity, for ninety-nine out of every hundred riders' ('From the Oranges', *Wheel*, XII [1887], p. 389).

31 Frances Melville Thomas to HM, 7 August 1886, *Writings*, vol. XIV, p. 734; Karl Kron, *Ten Thousand Miles on a Bicycle* (1887; New York, 1982), p. 112; [L. H. Porter], 'From the Oranges', *Wheel*, XII (1887), p. 422; Newell B. Woodworth, 'The Orange Athletic Club', *Outing*, XV (1889), pp. 124–30.

32 'Orange's Athletic Club', *New York Times*, 25 January 1887, p. 2.

33 'A Boom at the Berkeley A. C.', *Sun*, 5 March 1891, p. 4; HM to Abraham Lansing, 8 December 1880, *Writings*, vol. XIV, p. 475.

34 Kevin J. Hayes, *The Cambridge Introduction to Herman Melville* (Cambridge, 2007), pp. 100–103.

35 [Fitz-James O'Brien,] 'Our Young Authors: Melville', *Putnam's Monthly*, I (1853), p. 164.

36 Osborne, 'Childhood Recollections', p. 157.

37 Hershel Parker, *Herman Melville: A Biography* (Baltimore, MD, 1996–2002), vol. II, p. 889.

38 Ferris Greenslet, *Under the Bridge: An Autobiography* (Boston, MA, 1943); Merton M. Sealts Jr, 'Additions to the Early Lives of Melville', *Melville Society Extracts*, no. 28 (1976), pp. 12–13.

39 Huybertie Pruyn Hamlin, *An Albany Girlhood*, ed. Alice P. Kenney (Albany, NY, 1990), p. 170; Tip Roseberry, 'Mrs. Hamlin Knew Melville', *Times-Union*, 17 April 1952, p. 14.

40 Sealts, 'Additions', p. 11.

41 James Billson to HM, 21 August 1884, *Writings*, vol. XIV, p. 724.

42 W. Clark Russell to HM, 21 July 1886, *Writings*, vol. XIV, p. 731.

43 V. S. Pritchett, 'Without the Whale', *New Statesman*, 19 April 1958, p. 505.

44 Frederick James Kennedy and Joyce Deveau Kennedy, 'Archibald MacMechan and the Melville Revival', *Leviathan*, I (1999), p. 9; Kevin J. Hayes, 'Marcus Clarke and the Melville Revival', *Notes and Queries*, LXIII (2016), pp. 261–3.

Select Bibliography

Useful Editions of Melville's Work

Cohen, Hennig, ed., *The Battle-Pieces of Herman Melville* (New York, 1963)

—, ed., *Israel Potter: His Fifty Years of Exile* (New York, 1991)

Foster, Elizabeth S., ed., *The Confidence-Man: His Masquerade* (New York, 1954)

Hayford, Harrison, and Walter Blair, eds, *Omoo: A Narrative of Adventures in the South Seas* (New York, 1969)

—, and Merton M. Sealts Jr, eds, *Billy Budd, Sailor (An Inside Narrative): Reading Text and Genetic Text* (Chicago, IL, 1962)

—, G. Thomas Tanselle and Hershel Parker, eds, *The Writings of Herman Melville*, 14 vols to date (Evanston, IL, 1968–)

Humphreys, A. R., ed., *White-Jacket, or, The World in a Man-of-war* (London, 1966)

Leyda, Jay, ed., *The Complete Stories of Herman Melville* (New York, 1949)

Mansfield, Luther S., and Howard P. Vincent, eds, *Moby-Dick: or, The Whale* (New York, 1952)

Murray, Henry A., ed., *Pierre: or, The Ambiguities* (New York, 1962)

Parker, Hershel, ed., *Pierre: or, The Ambiguities* (New York, 1995)

Sadleir, Michael, ed., *The Works of Herman Melville*, 16 vols (London, 1922–4)

Sanborn, Geoffrey, ed., *Typee: Complete Text with Introduction, Historical Contexts, Critical Essays* (Boston, MA, 2004)

Thorp, Willard, ed., *Herman Melville: Representative Selections, with Introduction, Bibliography, and Notes* (New York, 1938)

Wright, Nathalia, ed., *Mardi, and A Voyage Thither* (Putney, VT, 1990)

Biographies

Freeman, John, *Herman Melville* (London, 1926)

Howard, Leon, *Herman Melville: A Biography* (Berkeley, CA, 1951)

Leyda, Jay, *The Melville Log: A Documentary Life of Herman Melville*, 2 vols
(New York, 1969)

Metcalf, Eleanor Melville, *Herman Melville, Cycle and Epicycle* (Cambridge,
MA, 1953)

Parker, Hershel, *Herman Melville: A Biography*, 2 vols (Baltimore, MD,
1996–2002)

Robertson-Lorant, Laurie, *Melville: A Biography* (New York, 1996)

Sealts, Merton M., Jr, *The Early Lives of Melville: Nineteenth-century
Biographical Sketches and their Authors* (Madison, WI, 1974)

Reference Works

Bercaw, Mary K., *Melville's Sources* (Evanston, IL, 1987)

Branch, Watson G., *Melville: The Critical Heritage* (London, 1974)

Coffler, Gail H., *Melville's Classical Allusions: A Comprehensive Index and
Glossary* (Westport, CT, 1985)

Cowen, Walker, *Melville's Marginalia*, 2 vols (New York, 1987)

Hayes, Kevin J., and Hershel Parker, *Checklist of Melville Reviews* (Evanston,
IL, 1991)

Higgins, Brian, *Herman Melville: An Annotated Bibliography* (Boston, MA,
1979)

—, *Herman Melville: A Reference Guide, 1931–1960* (Boston, MA, 1987)

Higgins, Brian, and Hershel Parker, eds, *Herman Melville: The Contemporary
Reviews* (Cambridge, 1995)

Olsen-Smith, Steven, ed., *Melville in His Own Time: A Biographical Chronicle
of His Life, Drawn from Recollections, Interviews, and Memoirs by Family,
Friends, and Associates* (Iowa City, IA, 2015)

Sealts, Merton M., Jr, *Melville's Reading*, revd edn (Columbia, SC, 1988)

Critical and Historical Studies

Anderson, Charles Roberts, *Melville in the South Seas* (New York, 1939)

Arvin, Newton, *Herman Melville* (New York, 1950)

Chase, Richard, *Herman Melville: A Critical Study* (New York, 1949)

Davis, Merrell R., *Melville's Mardi, A Chartless Voyage* (New Haven, CT, 1952)

Evelev, John, *Tolerable Entertainment: Herman Melville and Professionalism in Antebellum New York* (Amherst, NY, 2006)

Freeburg, Christopher, *Melville and the Idea of Blackness: Race and Imperialism in Nineteenth-century America* (Cambridge, 2012)

Garner, Stanton, *The Civil War World of Herman Melville* (Lawrence, KS, 1993)

Gilman, William H., *Melville's Early Life and Redburn* (New York, 1951)

Grey, Robin, *Melville and Milton: An Edition and Analysis of Melville's Annotations on Milton* (Pittsburgh, PA, 2004)

Hayes, Kevin J., *The Cambridge Introduction to Herman Melville* (Cambridge, 2007)

—, *Melville's Folk Roots* (Kent, OH, 1999)

Hayford, Harrison, *Melville's Prisoners* (Evanston, IL, 2003)

Heflin, Wilson L., *Herman Melville's Whaling Years*, ed. Mary K. Bercaw Edwards and Thomas Farel Heffernan (Nashville, TN, 2004)

Higgins, Brian, and Hershel Parker, *Reading Melville's Pierre; or, The Ambiguities* (Baton Rouge, LA, 2006)

Humphreys, A. R., *Melville* (Edinburgh, 1962)

James, C.L.R., *Mariners, Renegades, and Castaways: The Story of Herman Melville and the World We Live In* (New York, 1953)

Maloney, Ian S., *Melville's Monumental Imagination* (London, 2006)

Mayoux, Jean Jacques, *Melville*, trans. John Ashbery (New York, 1960)

Olson, Charles, *Collected Prose*, ed. Donald Allen and Benjamin Friedlander (Berkeley, CA, 1997)

Otter, Samuel, *Melville's Anatomies* (Berkeley, CA, 1999)

Parker, Hershel, *Melville Biography: An Inside Narrative* (Evanston, IL, 2012)

—, *Melville: The Making of the Poet* (Evanston, IL, 2008)

—, *Reading Billy Budd* (Evanston, IL, 1990)

Pommer, Henry F., *Milton and Melville* (Pittsburgh, PA, 1950)

Robillard, Douglas, *Melville and the Visual Arts: Ionian Form, Venetian Tint* (Kent, OH, 1997)

Rosenberry, Edward H., *Melville and the Comic Spirit* (Cambridge, MA, 1955)

Sanborn, Geoffrey, *The Sign of the Cannibal: Melville and the Making of a Postcolonial Reader* (Durham, NC, 1998)

Sealts, Merton M., Jr., *Pursuing Melville, 1940–1980: Chapters and Essays* (Madison, WI, 1982)

Seelye, John, *Melville: The Ironic Diagram* (Evanston, IL, 1970)

Stuckey, Sterling, *African Culture and Melville's Art: The Creative Process in Benito Cereno and Moby-Dick* (Oxford, 2009)

Thomson, Shawn, *The Romantic Architecture of Herman Melville's Moby-Dick* (Madison, NJ, 2001)

Vincent, Howard P., *The Tailoring of Melville's White-Jacket* (Evanston, IL, 1970)

—, *The Trying-out of Moby-Dick* (Carbondale, IL, 1949)

Wright, Nathalia, *Melville's Use of the Bible* (Durham, NC, 1949)

Yothers, Brian, *Sacred Uncertainty: Religious Difference and the Shape of Melville's Career* (Evanston, IL, 2015)

Young, Philip, *The Private Melville* (University Park, IL, 1993)

Acknowledgements

'All you have to do is put out your hand': so my teacher Hershel Parker used to say as he encouraged us students to search for new information that would contribute to our understanding of Herman Melville's life and works. Though thirty years have passed since I first heard these words, I still remember them and would like to thank Prof. Parker for his encouragement. I also thank Alfred Bendixen for organizing the American Literature Association Symposium on Biography in Puerto Vallarta. At this conference I was pleased to discuss the craft of biography with many other biographers. It is my general view that people have great memories for conversation, which many biographers have hesitated to use. I was pleased to meet other biographers at this conference who shared my conviction and who encouraged me to make use of remembered conversations recorded in reminiscences. I have not invented any dialogue for this book. Conversations reported here come from Melville's non-fiction writings or the letters and reminiscences of people who knew him personally. None of the reported conversations come from Melville's imaginative writings.

Many others deserve thanks. I especially thank Michael Leaman and Reaktion for inviting me to contribute to the Critical Lives series. David Bond of the Special Collections Research Center, Morris Library, Southern Illinois University, helped me with illustrations. Many other librarians have provided valuable assistance, including those at the Berkshire Athenaeum, the Berkshire Historical Society at Herman Melville's Arrowhead and the New York Public Library. The librarians at the Sanger Branch of the Toledo Lucas County Public Library also deserve my heartfelt thanks. During the composition of this book I made numerous requests from OhioLink, the statewide consortium of academic libraries, which the Sanger librarians filled kindly and expeditiously. As always, I thank my wife Myung-Sook, whose enthusiasm and curiosity have encouraged me to further my knowledge of Herman Melville and everything.

Photo Acknowledgements

The author and publishers wish to express their thanks to the below sources of illustrative material and/or permission to reproduce it:

Photos Bowling Green State University Library, Ohio: pp. 17, 120; photos William S. Carlson Library, University of Toledo, Toledo, OH: pp. 18, 61, 63, 74, 97, 103, 147, 149; collection of the author: pp. 77, 119, 125; photos Library of Congress, Washington, DC: pp. 6, 27, 31, 46, 47, 51, 72, 83, 86, 88, 89, 92, 100, 110, 113, 115, 116, 123, 131, 155, 157, 163, 164, 168, 174; photos Morris Library, Southern Illinois University, Carbondale, IL: p. 66.